Let Go 'N Live: A Guide to Releasing Stress and Finding Inner Peace

Bradford M. Smith

Copyright © 2024 Bradford M. Smith

All rights reserved.

ISBN: 9798341218888

Dedication:

To those who carry the weight of the world on their shoulders,
May you find the strength to let go,
the courage to embrace change,
and the peace that comes from living fully in the present.
This book is dedicated to everyone who seeks freedom from their burdens,
to all who choose compassion over perfection,
and to those brave enough to surrender to life's uncertainties.
May you let go and truly live.

TABLE OF CONTENTS

Introduction: Welcome to Let Go 'N Live

Chapter 1: The Power of Letting Go

Chapter 2: Cultivating Mindfulness

Chapter 3: Letting Go of Perfectionism

Chapter 4: Creating Space for Yourself

Chapter 5: The Power of Forgiveness

Chapter 6: Embracing Change

Chapter 7: Building Resilience Through Self-Care

Chapter 8: Cultivating Gratitude for a Resilient and Joyful Life

Conclusion: Living Fully Through Letting Go

Expanded Workbook: Practical Tools for Intentional Living, Personal Growth, Mindfulness and Letting Go

References

Acknowledgements

About The Author

Introduction: Welcome to Let Go 'N Live

In the modern world, we are constantly bombarded with messages that tell us to achieve more, be more, and never stop pushing. We are told that success comes from holding tight to our dreams, working endlessly, and never letting go of our goals. But what if the key to happiness and fulfillment is not found in holding on tighter, but in letting go?

This book, *Let Go 'N Live*, is about freeing yourself from the emotional, mental, and physical burdens that come from gripping too tightly to things that no longer serve you. Whether it's perfectionism, stress, resentment, fear, or the need for control, letting go can help you find the peace, joy, and fulfillment that has always been within you.

Section 1: The Problem with Holding On

We hold onto things—stress, control, expectations, grudges—because we think they keep us safe. We believe that by controlling outcomes, by demanding perfection from ourselves and others, or by holding onto resentment, we can protect ourselves from pain, failure, or disappointment. Yet the irony is that the more tightly we hold on, the more we feel overwhelmed, anxious, and disconnected from ourselves and the world around us.

Consider how your body feels when you're stressed. Your shoulders tighten, your heart rate increases, and your mind races with "what ifs" and worst-case scenarios. Now think about how it feels when you've let go of a worry or fear that's been haunting you. There's a sense of lightness, of relief, of finally being able to breathe again. This contrast shows us that clinging to things—whether it's control, fear, or anger—creates physical and emotional weight that holds us back from living fully.

Modern life is filled with pressures that exacerbate this tendency to hold on. Social media encourages constant comparison. Workplaces demand productivity without pause. Relationships sometimes become battlegrounds where we fight for control or validation. We live in a culture that often confuses busyness with worthiness, control with strength, and perfection with success.

But what if the very things we think will protect us—like perfectionism, control, and busyness—are actually the things preventing us from experiencing true peace and happiness?

Section 2: The Cost of Holding On

To understand why letting go is so powerful, we first need to recognize the cost of holding on.

Emotional Cost: When we hold onto perfectionism, we are never satisfied with ourselves. There is always something we could have done better, a goal we didn't achieve, or an outcome that didn't match our expectations. This constant striving for perfection keeps us in a state of anxiety, fear, and self-criticism. We never give ourselves permission to be flawed, to make mistakes, or to simply be human.

When we cling to grudges and resentment, we tie ourselves to past pain. Holding onto anger doesn't punish the person who hurt us—it punishes us. It keeps us in a cycle of bitterness, preventing us from experiencing joy or moving forward. As **Nelson Mandela** once said, "Resentment is like drinking poison and then hoping it will kill your enemies."

Mental Cost: Clinging to control is mentally exhausting. When we believe that we need to control every outcome—whether in our work, relationships, or personal lives—we are constantly on edge, ready to react to any unexpected event. This mental load weighs us down, creating burnout and diminishing our ability to be present in the moment.

We spend so much time anticipating problems, planning contingencies, and worrying about things that may never happen that we miss the opportunities for joy and connection that are happening right now. **Brené Brown** speaks to this in her work on vulnerability, noting that we often numb ourselves to joy out of fear that something will go wrong. We can't fully embrace happiness because we are too busy bracing for the next challenge.

Physical Cost: Holding onto stress, control, and perfectionism doesn't just affect our emotional and mental well-being—it has profound effects on our physical health. Research shows that chronic stress increases cortisol levels, weakens the immune system, and is linked to conditions like heart disease, anxiety disorders, and depression. When we are constantly in a state of fight-or-flight, our bodies never get the chance to relax, repair, and recover.

The act of letting go, on the other hand, has been shown to reduce cortisol levels, lower blood pressure, and increase feelings of well-being. **Jon Kabat-**

Zinn, a pioneer in mindfulness-based stress reduction, has demonstrated that mindfulness and letting go of stress can literally change the brain, reducing activity in areas associated with anxiety and increasing gray matter in regions related to emotional regulation and empathy.

Section 3: The Benefits of Letting Go

Letting go isn't about giving up. It's not about becoming passive or disengaged from life. In fact, it's the opposite. Letting go is about releasing what no longer serves you so that you can live more fully and authentically. It's about trusting yourself, trusting the process of life, and allowing things to unfold without constantly trying to force or control them.

Emotional Freedom: Letting go of perfectionism allows you to embrace self-compassion. Instead of constantly judging yourself for not being "enough," you can accept yourself as you are. **Dr. Kristin Neff**, a leading researcher on self-compassion, explains that when we are kind to ourselves, we build emotional resilience and are better able to navigate life's challenges. By letting go of the need to be perfect, we open ourselves to learning, growth, and joy.

Letting go of resentment frees us from the grip of the past. It allows us to forgive—not because the person who hurt us deserves forgiveness, but because we deserve peace. As **Maya Angelou** beautifully stated, "You may not control all the events that happen to you, but you can decide not to be reduced by them."

Mental Clarity: When we let go of the need to control everything, we free up mental space for creativity, problem-solving, and genuine connection. Letting go of control doesn't mean we stop caring or trying; it means we trust ourselves enough to adapt to whatever comes our way, rather than being fixated on one particular outcome.

Physical Well-being: As we let go of stress and tension, our bodies begin to heal. Letting go allows our nervous systems to shift from a state of constant arousal (fight-or-flight) to one of rest and restoration. This reduces the physical toll of stress and improves our overall health.

Section 4: What You Will Learn in This Book
In *Let Go 'N Live*, you will learn how to release the things that hold you back and embrace a life filled with more peace, joy, and presence. Each chapter will

guide you through a different aspect of letting go, offering practical tools, reflections, and exercises to help you integrate these practices into your daily life.

- **Chapter 1** will explore the *Power of Letting Go*. You'll learn why we cling to things that no longer serve us and how to start releasing the emotional baggage that weighs us down.

- **Chapter 2** will focus on *Mindfulness*, providing you with tools to cultivate awareness and presence in your everyday life. You'll discover how mindfulness can help you release stress, worry, and mental clutter.

- **Chapter 3** will guide you in *Letting Go of Perfectionism*. You'll explore the roots of perfectionism and learn how to embrace imperfection, self-compassion, and authenticity.

- **Chapter 4** will teach you how to *Create Space for Yourself*. By decluttering your environment, mind, and schedule, you'll make room for what truly matters.

- **Chapter 5** will delve into the transformative power of *Forgiveness*. You'll learn how to let go of resentment and past hurts, opening yourself up to healing and peace.

- **Chapter 6** will show you how to *Embrace Change*. Instead of resisting life's inevitable transitions, you'll learn to flow with them, trusting that change is a natural and essential part of growth.

- **Chapter 7** will help you build *Resilience Through Self-Care*. You'll create a personalized self-care routine that nourishes your body, mind, and spirit, helping you let go of burnout and exhaustion.

- **Chapter 8** will explore the connection between *Cultivating Gratitude for a Resilient and Joyful Life*. You'll discover how letting go of attachment and cultivating gratitude can bring you a deeper sense of purpose and connection.

Finally, the **Conclusion** will tie all these elements together, reinforcing the idea that letting go is not a one-time event, but a lifelong practice. You'll also find an **Expanded Workbook**, with practical exercises, journaling prompts, and rituals to help you implement the lessons from the book into your daily life.

Section 5: The Journey Ahead
The journey of letting go is deeply personal. There will be moments when it feels liberating and joyful, and other times when it feels uncomfortable and challenging. This is normal. Letting go isn't about avoiding discomfort—it's about facing it with grace and courage.

As you move through this book, remember that letting go is a process. It doesn't happen overnight, and it's not something you can check off your to-do list. It's an ongoing practice of releasing what no longer serves you so that you can make space for what truly matters.

You deserve to live a life free from unnecessary burdens. You deserve to experience joy, peace, and fulfillment. By learning to let go, you are giving yourself permission to live fully and authentically.

Let go, and live.

Chapter 1: The Power of Letting Go

Introduction to Letting Go

Letting go is one of the most powerful acts of self-liberation we can undertake. It requires courage, self-awareness, and the willingness to release what no longer serves us. For many, the idea of letting go feels like giving up, losing control, or surrendering to chaos. But the truth is, letting go is about creating space for what truly matters—peace, joy, love, and authenticity.

In this chapter, we will explore why we hold on so tightly to things like fear, stress, resentment, and perfectionism, and how doing so keeps us trapped in cycles of pain, anxiety, and disappointment. We will then delve into the profound benefits of letting go, offering you practical tools to begin releasing the emotional and mental burdens that weigh you down.

By the end of this chapter, you'll have a clearer understanding of why letting go is essential to living a fulfilled, authentic life and how you can start incorporating it into your daily existence.

Section 1: Understanding Why We Hold On

The first step to letting go is understanding why we hold on in the first place. At the core of most of our attachments—whether it's to expectations, control, or resentment—is fear. We fear uncertainty, failure, rejection, and loss. And so, we hold on tightly to the things we believe will keep us safe and secure.

1.1 The Role of Fear

Fear of the Unknown: Humans are wired to seek certainty and avoid risk. Our brains are designed to protect us from danger, but in the modern world, this survival mechanism often backfires. We hold onto relationships, jobs, or habits not because they serve us, but because they are familiar. Letting go of these things requires us to step into the unknown, which can feel terrifying. As psychologist **Susan Jeffers** famously said, "Feel the fear and do it anyway." Acknowledging fear is the first step in overcoming it.

Fear of Failure: Many of us hold onto perfectionism or control because we fear failure. We believe that if we can just control every variable, we can prevent mistakes, avoid judgment, and guarantee success. However, this need for control is not only exhausting, it's also impossible. Failure is a natural part of growth and learning, and when we accept this, we can begin to let go of the unrealistic expectations we place on ourselves.

Fear of Rejection: Holding onto relationships or personas that no longer align with who we are is often driven by the fear of rejection. We fear that if we show our true selves—our vulnerabilities, flaws, and imperfections—others will reject us. But as **Brené Brown** has demonstrated in her research on vulnerability, true connection and love can only exist when we embrace our imperfections and show up authentically.

1.2 The Illusion of Control

The Need for Control: One of the main reasons we hold on is because we believe that control gives us power and safety. We try to control our circumstances, our relationships, and even our emotions, believing that if we manage every detail, we can prevent bad things from happening. But as much as we might want to believe otherwise, control is an illusion. The reality is that life is unpredictable, and the more we try to control it, the more we feel stressed, anxious, and disconnected.

Letting go of control doesn't mean giving up or being passive. It means accepting that we can't control everything and trusting that we have the resilience and strength to handle whatever comes our way.

Section 2: The Cost of Holding On

Holding on to fear, stress, and control comes at a high cost—mentally, emotionally, and physically.

2.1 Emotional Cost
When we hold onto resentment, anger, or grudges, we create emotional blocks that prevent us from experiencing joy, love, and peace. **Nelson Mandela** once said, "Resentment is like drinking poison and then hoping it will kill your enemies." When we hold onto anger or hurt, we aren't punishing the person who wronged us; we are punishing ourselves. The emotional toll of holding onto past hurts can manifest as chronic stress, anxiety, depression, and even physical illness.

2.2 Mental Cost

Mentally, holding on creates a state of constant tension. When we are fixated on controlling outcomes or avoiding failure, our minds are in a perpetual state of overdrive. We become preoccupied with "what if" scenarios, constantly trying to anticipate and prevent negative outcomes. This mental load is exhausting and robs us of the ability to be present. It diminishes our capacity for creativity, problem-solving, and genuine connection with others. **Psychologist and author Daniel Goleman** explains that when we are stressed or anxious, our brain's prefrontal cortex—the part responsible for rational thought and decision-making—is less effective. This leads to more impulsive, reactive behavior and impairs our ability to think clearly and make sound decisions.

2.3 Physical Cost

Holding on to stress, anger, or control has significant physical consequences as well. Chronic stress elevates cortisol levels, which can weaken the immune system, increase blood pressure, and lead to heart disease. According to research from the **American Psychological Association**, people who are under chronic stress are more likely to experience sleep disturbances, digestive problems, and headaches.

On the other hand, letting go of stress and control has been shown to reduce cortisol levels and improve overall well-being. **Jon Kabat-Zinn**, a pioneer in mindfulness-based stress reduction (MBSR), has demonstrated through numerous studies that practicing mindfulness and letting go of stress can have profound effects on both mental and physical health. When we let go of stress, we allow our bodies to enter a state of relaxation, which promotes healing, restoration, and balance.

Section 3: The Benefits of Letting Go

Letting go is not about giving up. It's about freeing ourselves from the emotional, mental, and physical burdens that weigh us down. When we let go, we create space for joy, love, creativity, and connection. Here are some of the profound benefits of letting go:

3.1 Emotional Freedom
Letting go of perfectionism, control, and resentment allows us to experience emotional freedom. Instead of constantly judging ourselves or others, we can embrace self-compassion and acceptance. **Dr. Kristin Neff**, a leading researcher on self-compassion, explains that when we are kind to ourselves, we build emotional resilience and are better able to navigate life's challenges. When we let go of the need to be perfect, we give ourselves permission to be human. We no longer see mistakes as failures, but as opportunities to learn and grow. This shift in mindset allows us to approach life with more curiosity, playfulness, and openness.

3.2 Mental Clarity

When we let go of the need to control everything, we free up mental space for creativity, problem-solving, and connection. Letting go allows us to be more present, which enhances our ability to think clearly and make decisions from a place of calm and confidence.

Mindfulness practices, such as meditation, have been shown to improve focus, attention, and cognitive flexibility. When we are no longer consumed by stress or anxiety, we can approach challenges with a clearer, more balanced mind.

3.3 Physical Well-being

Letting go of stress and tension has profound effects on our physical health. As release the need to control everything, our bodies shift from a state of fight-or-flight to a state of rest and relaxation. This allows our nervous system to return to balance, reducing the physical toll of chronic stress.
Research shows that mindfulness and letting go practices can improve sleep quality, lower blood pressure, and boost the immune system. When we let go of stress, our bodies can heal, restore, and thrive.

Section 4: Practical Strategies for Letting Go

Now that we've explored why we hold on and the benefits of letting go, let's dive into some practical strategies that you can start using today to release stress, fear, and control.

4.1 Mindfulness Meditation

One of the most effective ways to let go is through mindfulness meditation. By practicing mindfulness, we train our minds to observe thoughts and emotions without attaching to them. This allows us to let go of stressful or negative thoughts before they spiral out of control.

Exercise: Set aside 10 minutes each day to practice mindfulness meditation. Sit in a comfortable position, close your eyes, and focus on your breath. When thoughts arise (and they will), simply observe them without judgment and gently return your focus to your breath. Over time, this practice will help you develop the ability to let go of thoughts and emotions that don't serve you.

4.2 Journaling

Writing is a powerful tool for letting go. When we write down our fears, worries, or resentments, we externalize them, making it easier to release them.

Exercise: Try this simple journaling exercise called the "Letting Go Letter." Write a letter to yourself or someone who has hurt you, expressing everything you've been holding onto. Don't hold back—this is for your eyes only. After you've written the letter, tear it up, burn it, or dispose of it in a way that symbolizes releasing the burden.

4.3 Self-Compassion

Letting go of perfectionism requires cultivating self-compassion. The next time you catch yourself being overly critical or demanding of yourself, pause and ask, "Would I say this to a close friend?" If the answer is no, reframe the thought with kindness.

Exercise: Create a list of compassionate affirmations you can use when you feel overwhelmed or inadequate.

4.4 Letting Go of Perfectionism Through Self-Compassion

One of the most challenging aspects of letting go is releasing the deeply ingrained belief that we need to be perfect. Society often rewards perfectionism, equating it with success, competence, and value. However, perfectionism is a heavy burden that keeps us from living authentically and joyfully. Letting go of perfectionism begins with practicing self-compassion.

When we release the idea that we must be flawless, we open ourselves up to vulnerability, connection, and growth. **Dr. Kristin Neff**, a pioneer in self-compassion research, explains that self-compassion allows us to accept ourselves with kindness, even when we make mistakes or fall short of our expectations.

Exercise:
- **Self-Compassion Journaling**: The next time you experience failure or feel like you're not living up to your expectations, take out your journal and write about the situation from a compassionate perspective. Imagine you're speaking to a dear friend who is struggling. What would you say to them? How would you comfort and encourage them? Now, write those same words to yourself. This exercise helps shift your inner dialogue from one of criticism to one of understanding and care.

4.5 Releasing Resentment Through Forgiveness

Resentment is one of the most toxic forms of emotional holding on. When we harbor resentment, we are tied to the person or situation that caused us pain, unable to move forward. Forgiveness doesn't mean condoning the wrong or forgetting what happened. It means releasing the hold that the hurt has on you, allowing you to move forward with peace.

Forgiveness is not for them—it's for you. As **Desmond Tutu** wisely said, "Forgiveness says you are given another chance to make a new beginning." By letting go of resentment, we free ourselves from the past and create space for healing and joy.

Exercise:
- **The Forgiveness Letter**: Think of someone you are holding a grudge against or feel unresolved anger toward. Write a letter to this person, detailing your feelings—what hurt you, how it affected you, and why you've held onto the pain. Then, in the letter, express your willingness to forgive them, not because they necessarily deserve it, but because you deserve peace. You do not have to send the letter. The act of writing it is the release.

4.6 Visualization for Letting Go

Visualization is a powerful tool for letting go of mental and emotional clutter. It engages your imagination, helping you symbolically release the things you've been holding onto. This technique can be particularly effective for letting go of fear, anxiety, and the need for control.

Exercise:
- **The Balloon Visualization**: Sit comfortably and close your eyes. Take a few deep breaths to relax. Now, imagine holding a balloon in your hand. Inside the balloon is whatever you want to let go of—whether it's a fear, a grudge, or an expectation. Visualize the color and shape of the balloon. When you're ready, imagine yourself releasing the balloon and watching it float away into the sky. As it drifts farther away, imagine the burden of what you were holding onto becoming lighter and lighter. When the balloon disappears from sight, take a moment to breathe deeply and feel the lightness in your body.

4.7 Setting Boundaries to Let Go of External Pressures

A major reason we hold onto stress is that we often say "yes" when we really want to say "no." We take on more than we can handle, often out of a desire to please others, avoid conflict, or meet external expectations. Learning to set boundaries is an essential part of letting go of stress, overcommitment, and burnout.

Setting boundaries is an act of self-respect. It allows us to protect our energy and focus on what truly matters. As we learn to set and maintain boundaries, we let go of the need to be everything to everyone and begin honoring our own needs.

Exercise:
- **The Boundary Audit**: Take a moment to reflect on your current commitments—whether they are related to work, family, friends, or community. Write down any areas where you feel overextended or resentful of the demands placed on you. Now, for each of these areas, write down one boundary you can set to protect your time and energy. For example, if you find yourself constantly responding to work emails after hours, set a boundary by turning off email notifications at a certain time each evening. Reflect on how setting this boundary will allow you to let go of unnecessary stress and reclaim your well-being.

4.8 Decluttering Your Physical Space

Just as we can hold onto emotional baggage, we often hold onto physical clutter that weighs us down. Our surroundings greatly impact our mental and emotional state. A cluttered environment can create feelings of overwhelm, stress, and confusion, while a clean, organized space can promote clarity, calm, and focus.

Marie Kondo, author of *The Life-Changing Magic of Tidying Up*, teaches that decluttering is not just about getting rid of things—it's about making space for what truly sparks joy in your life. By letting go of possessions that no longer serve a purpose, you create a more peaceful and intentional living space.

Exercise:
- **Declutter Your Space**: Choose one area of your home that feels cluttered or chaotic. It could be your bedroom, your office, or even just a drawer. Spend 30 minutes decluttering this space—getting rid of items you no longer use, organizing what you want to keep, and creating a sense of order. As you do this, pay attention to how you feel. Does clearing physical space help you feel mentally lighter? Reflect on how letting go of material clutter opens up space for peace

and simplicity in your life.

Section 5: Letting Go as a Lifelong Practice

Letting go is not something you do once and then move on from. It is a lifelong practice—something you must return to again and again. There will be moments when you feel light and free, and other moments when old fears, anxieties, or habits creep back in. This is normal. The key is not to view letting go as a one-time event but as an ongoing process of release, reflection, and renewal.

5.1 Embracing Impermanence

One of the core teachings in both Buddhism and mindfulness practices is the concept of impermanence. Everything in life is constantly changing—our thoughts, emotions, relationships, and circumstances. When we cling to the idea of permanence, we create suffering. But when we embrace the truth of impermanence, we can flow with life's changes rather than resist them.

Thich Nhat Hanh, the renowned Zen Buddhist monk, often teaches that letting go is the pathway to freedom because it allows us to live in harmony with life's natural rhythms. "You must love in such a way that the person you love feels free," he said, reminding us that love and freedom go hand in hand.

Exercise:
- **Impermanence Meditation**: Set aside 10 minutes to meditate on the concept of impermanence. Sit quietly and bring to mind something in your life that is changing—this could be a relationship, a job, or a personal situation. Instead of resisting or fearing this change, allow yourself to breathe into it. As you inhale, acknowledge the impermanence of this moment. As you exhale, let go of your need to control it. With each breath, remind yourself that everything is temporary, and that accepting change is the key to peace.

5.2 Returning to Your Practice

Even as you make progress in letting go, you may find yourself slipping back into old patterns of holding on. This is part of the process. Life will continue to challenge you with opportunities to practice letting go—whether it's letting go of a past hurt, a desire for control, or a fear of the future.

The most important thing is to be gentle with yourself. Letting go is not about perfection; it's about progress. Each time you return to the practice, you strengthen your ability to release what no longer serves you.

Exercise:
- **Monthly Reflection**: At the end of each month, take time to reflect on your journey of letting go. Write down one thing you successfully let go of and one area where you still struggle. Acknowledge the progress you've made and set a small, achievable intention for the month ahead. For example, if you've let go of resentment in one area of your life, but still struggle with perfectionism, your intention might be to practice self-compassion in moments of stress.

Conclusion to Chapter 1: The Freedom of Letting Go

Letting go is one of the greatest acts of self-love. It is a practice that allows you to release the burdens that weigh you down—whether they are emotional, mental, or physical—and make space for peace, joy, and freedom. By letting go of fear, perfectionism, control, and resentment, you open the door to living fully and authentically.

As we conclude this chapter, it's important to reflect on how letting go isn't a single act but a daily practice. By recognizing and releasing the things that no longer serve us—whether they are outdated beliefs, unhelpful habits, or emotions like fear, anger, and perfectionism—we can live a life that is lighter, more joyful, and authentically aligned with our true values.

Letting go is about embracing what is, rather than clinging to what we wish would be. It's about acknowledging that we cannot control every outcome or predict every turn life will take. And yet, there is immense freedom in that realization. When we let go of control, we begin to trust ourselves, the process, and the unfolding of our journey. It is in this space of surrender that we find true peace.

This chapter has laid the foundation for the work ahead, helping you understand the "why" behind letting go and offering practical tools to start incorporating this powerful practice into your life. In the chapters to come, we will deepen this exploration, providing more specific strategies for letting go in different areas of life—whether it's through cultivating mindfulness, releasing perfectionism, or embracing change.

But as you continue on this path, always remember: Letting go is not about loss. It is about creating space for what truly matters.

Chapter 2: Cultivating Mindfulness

Introduction to Mindfulness and Letting Go

Mindfulness is the cornerstone of letting go. It allows us to be fully present in the moment, without being weighed down by worries about the past or anxieties about the future. When we practice mindfulness, we cultivate awareness of our thoughts, feelings, and physical sensations without attaching to them or letting them dictate our behavior.

At its core, mindfulness is about observation without judgment. Instead of reacting to our thoughts and emotions, we learn to simply observe them. This practice is essential for letting go because it creates the space we need to recognize when we are holding onto something unnecessarily.

In this chapter, we will explore how to develop a mindfulness practice that will help you release stress, let go of unhelpful thought patterns, and cultivate a deeper sense of peace and presence in your daily life.

Section 1: The Science of Mindfulness
Mindfulness is more than just a spiritual practice—it's also supported by a wealth of scientific research that demonstrates its profound impact on both mental and physical well-being.

1.1 The Neuroscience of Mindfulness

Mindfulness has been shown to physically change the brain. Studies conducted by **Dr. Sara Lazar** at Harvard University have revealed that consistent mindfulness practice increases gray matter in regions of the brain associated with memory, emotional regulation, and empathy, while decreasing activity in the amygdala, the part of the brain responsible for the fight-or-flight response.

This means that mindfulness can actually help reduce stress and improve emotional balance by rewiring the brain. When we are mindful, we are less likely to react impulsively to stressful situations and more likely to respond with calm and clarity.

1.2 Mindfulness and Emotional Regulation

One of the key benefits of mindfulness is its ability to help us regulate our emotions. Rather than being swept away by feelings of anger, anxiety, or sadness, mindfulness allows us to observe these emotions from a place of detachment. This doesn't mean ignoring or suppressing our emotions—it means creating space to feel them fully without being overwhelmed by them.

Research from Dr. Jon Kabat-Zinn, who developed the Mindfulness-Based Stress Reduction (MBSR) program, has shown that practicing mindfulness can significantly reduce symptoms of anxiety and depression. By becoming aware of our thoughts and emotions in a non-judgmental way, we are able to break the cycle of rumination and emotional reactivity that so often contributes to stress and mental health challenges.

Section 2: Building a Mindfulness Practice

Cultivating mindfulness is a practice, and like any skill, it requires consistency and patience. But the beauty of mindfulness is that it can be practiced anywhere, at any time. You don't need special equipment, a quiet room, or even a lot of time. You just need your breath and your attention.

2.1 Mindful Breathing

Mindful breathing is one of the simplest and most effective ways to anchor yourself in the present moment. By focusing on your breath, you can calm your nervous system and create space between your thoughts and your reactions.

Exercise: The 4-7-8 Breath

- **Instructions**: Sit in a comfortable position with your back straight. Close your eyes and take a deep breath in through your nose for a count of four. Hold the breath for a count of seven, and then slowly exhale through your mouth for a count of eight. Repeat this cycle for five to ten minutes.
- **Reflection**: After practicing mindful breathing, notice how your body and mind feel. Are you more relaxed? Less anxious? How did focusing on your breath help you let go of distractions and worries?

2.2 Body Scan Meditation

The body scan meditation is a practice that involves bringing attention to each part of your body, from your head to your toes, noticing any tension or discomfort without judgment. This practice helps you release physical tension and become more aware of how stress manifests in your body.

Exercise: Body Scan Meditation
- **Instructions**: Lie down in a comfortable position and close your eyes. Starting with your toes, bring your awareness to each part of your body, moving up through your legs, hips, back, arms, shoulders, neck, and head. As you focus on each area, notice any sensations of tension or discomfort and imagine releasing that tension with each exhale. Spend at least 15 minutes in this practice.
- **Reflection**: After completing the body scan, reflect on how your body feels. Did you notice areas of tension that you were previously unaware of? How did the act of bringing awareness to these areas help you let go of physical stress?

Section 3: Mindfulness in Daily Life

Mindfulness is not just something we practice on a meditation cushion or during quiet moments of reflection. It is a way of being in the world—a practice we can carry into every aspect of our lives.

3.1 Mindful Eating

Eating is something we often do mindlessly—scarfing down a meal while scrolling through our phones or rushing through a snack in between meetings. But when we bring mindfulness to the act of eating, it becomes a rich sensory experience that nourishes both body and mind.

Exercise: Mindful Eating
- **Instructions**: The next time you sit down for a meal, put away all distractions (phones, TV, etc.) and focus entirely on the act of eating. Pay attention to the texture, flavor, and aroma of the food. Take small bites and chew slowly, savoring each mouthful. Notice how the food feels in your mouth and how your body responds as you eat.
- **Reflection**: After the meal, reflect on how the experience of mindful eating differed from your usual habits. Did you notice a difference in how the food tasted or how satisfied you felt? How can you incorporate mindful eating into your daily routine?

3.2 Mindful Walking

Walking is another activity we often do on autopilot, rushing from one place to the next without paying much attention. Mindful walking is the practice of bringing full awareness to each step, turning a simple walk into a meditative experience.

Exercise: Mindful Walking
- **Instructions**: Choose a time each day to go for a walk, whether it's a short stroll around your neighborhood or a longer walk in a park. As you walk, focus on the sensation of your feet touching the ground, the movement of your body, and the rhythm of your breath. Notice the sounds, sights, and smells around you, staying fully present with each step.
- **Reflection**: After your walk, reflect on how mindful walking helped you feel more grounded and present. Did you notice things in your environment that you usually overlook? How did focusing on your breath and steps help you let go of distractions or worries?

Section 4: Overcoming Obstacles to Mindfulness

As you begin to integrate mindfulness into your life, you may encounter some common obstacles. These challenges are a normal part of the process, and it's important not to judge yourself when they arise.

4.1 Dealing with Distraction

One of the biggest challenges to mindfulness is the tendency for the mind to wander. It's easy to get caught up in thoughts about the past or worries about the future, even when you're trying to be present. The key is not to fight these distractions but to gently guide your attention back to the present moment each time you notice your mind drifting.

Exercise: Labeling Thoughts
- **Instructions**: The next time you practice mindfulness, try labeling your thoughts as they arise. For example, if you notice your mind wandering to your to-do list, simply label the thought "planning" and gently bring your attention back to your breath. If you notice a judgmental thought, label it "judgment" and return to your breath.
- **Reflection**: Reflect on how labeling thoughts helped you distance yourself from them. Did it make it easier to let go of distractions? How can this practice help you maintain focus during challenging moments?

4.2 Cultivating Patience

Mindfulness requires practice, and with practice comes patience. Often, we approach meditation or mindfulness exercises with the expectation of immediate results—expecting peace and calm after just a few sessions. But mindfulness is not about forcing an outcome. It's about showing up consistently, allowing whatever arises to surface, and meeting it with acceptance.

When you cultivate patience, you allow yourself to experience the present moment without the pressure of perfection. The key to successful mindfulness practice is to let go of the need for immediate results. It's okay if your mind wanders or if you don't feel immediate relief from stress or anxiety.

Exercise: The Practice of Patience
- **Instructions**: The next time you sit down to practice mindfulness—whether it's meditation, mindful breathing, or another technique—set the intention to simply *be present*, without any expectations. If thoughts arise about how well or poorly you are "doing" the practice, gently bring your awareness back to your breath. Remember, mindfulness is not about "doing it right" but about being open to what is.
- **Reflection**: After your practice, reflect on how setting an intention of patience affected your experience. Did it help you feel more at ease or less pressured? How can this mindset of patience be applied to other areas of your life where you feel impatient or rushed?

4.3 Letting Go of Judgment

One of the most common obstacles in mindfulness practice is judgment. We often approach mindfulness with the idea that we're supposed to feel a certain way, achieve a certain state of calm, or clear our minds of all thoughts. When that doesn't happen, we become frustrated or critical of ourselves.

Letting go of judgment means accepting each moment as it is, without labeling it as "good" or "bad." It's about allowing yourself to experience whatever arises—whether that's calm, frustration, distraction, or peace—without trying to change or fix it.

Exercise: Non-Judgmental Awareness
- **Instructions**: For your next mindfulness session, commit to practicing non-judgmental awareness. This means that whatever thoughts, emotions, or sensations arise, you simply acknowledge them without labeling them as positive or negative. For example, if you feel restless, instead of thinking, "I shouldn't be feeling this way,"

simply acknowledge, "There's restlessness here," and return to your breath.
- **Reflection**: Reflect on how letting go of judgment impacted your mindfulness practice. Did it help you feel more accepting of your experience? How might this practice of non-judgment carry over into your everyday life, particularly in how you judge yourself or others?

Section 5: Expanding Mindfulness into Everyday Life

Mindfulness is not just about sitting still in meditation; it's a way of living. The more you practice mindfulness, the more you can integrate it into your daily routine—whether that's during conversations, while you work, or even while doing mundane tasks like washing the dishes. Every moment presents an opportunity to practice presence.

5.1 Mindfulness in Conversations

Many of us have conversations on autopilot. We listen just enough to formulate a response while our minds race ahead, thinking about what we want to say next or anticipating where the conversation will go. Mindful listening, however, is the practice of being fully present with the person you are speaking to, giving them your complete attention without distraction or judgment.

Exercise: Mindful Listening
- **Instructions**: The next time you engage in a conversation, practice mindful listening. Set the intention to be fully present, giving the speaker your undivided attention. Avoid interrupting, planning your response, or letting your mind wander. Instead, focus on what the other person is saying, noticing their words, tone, and body language. When it's your turn to speak, respond from a place of genuine presence.
- **Reflection**: After the conversation, reflect on how mindful listening impacted the interaction. Did you notice anything different about how you felt during the conversation? How did the other person respond to your presence? How can this practice enhance your relationships?

5.2 Mindfulness in Routine Tasks

Many of the tasks we perform each day—like washing dishes, brushing our teeth, or commuting to work—are done mindlessly. We often rush through them, our minds elsewhere, thinking about what's next on our to-do list. But these routine tasks offer valuable opportunities for practicing mindfulness.

Exercise: Mindfulness in Daily Tasks

- **Instructions**: Choose one daily task—such as washing dishes, folding laundry, or brushing your teeth—and turn it into a mindfulness practice. As you perform the task, bring your full attention to the sensations, movements, and sounds involved. For example, if you're washing dishes, focus on the temperature of the water, the texture of the sponge, and the sound of the water running. Let go of thoughts about what you need to do next and focus solely on the present moment.
- **Reflection**: After completing the task mindfully, reflect on how the experience felt different from when you typically do it on autopilot. Did slowing down and focusing on the present moment affect your mood or sense of calm? How can you apply mindfulness to more daily tasks?

5.3 Mindfulness at Work

Work can be a source of stress and distraction, especially when we feel overwhelmed by deadlines, meetings, or responsibilities. Practicing mindfulness at work can help you stay focused, reduce stress, and increase your productivity by bringing more intentionality and presence to your tasks.

Exercise: Mindfulness at Your Desk

- **Instructions**: Set a timer for 5 minutes during your workday and take a mindful pause. Close your eyes (or soften your gaze), take a few deep breaths, and bring your attention to the present moment. Notice the feeling of your body sitting in the chair, the sounds around you, and the rhythm of your breath. Let go of any thoughts about what you need to do next, and simply be present. When the timer goes off, gently return to your work, bringing the same sense of focus and presence to your tasks.
- **Reflection**: After your mindful pause, reflect on how it impacted your ability to concentrate and manage stress. Did you feel more grounded or focused after taking a break for mindfulness? How can you incorporate mindful pauses throughout your workday to reduce stress and enhance productivity?

Section 6: The Long-Term Benefits of Mindfulness

The benefits of mindfulness grow over time. While the immediate effects of mindfulness—such as relaxation and focus—are valuable, the long-term benefits are even more profound. With consistent practice, mindfulness can help you develop greater emotional resilience, improve your relationships, and enhance your overall sense of well-being.

6.1 Emotional Resilience

When practiced regularly, mindfulness builds emotional resilience—the ability to navigate life's challenges with greater ease and balance. Instead of reacting impulsively to stressful situations, you learn to respond thoughtfully, creating space between stimulus and reaction.

Case Study: Emotional Resilience Through Mindfulness
- **Example**: A person who consistently practices mindfulness finds that during a heated argument, instead of immediately reacting with anger, they take a deep breath and pause. This moment of pause allows them to approach the situation with calm and clarity, leading to a more constructive conversation.
- **Reflection**: Think about a recent situation where you reacted impulsively. How might practicing mindfulness have changed your response? How can building emotional resilience through mindfulness help you handle future challenges with greater calm and composure?

6.2 Deepening Relationships

Mindfulness not only benefits your internal world but also enhances your relationships. When you are present with others—whether in conversations, shared activities, or during conflict—you build stronger, more authentic connections. Mindful communication fosters trust, empathy, and understanding.

Case Study: Deepening Connections with Mindfulness
- **Example**: A couple practices mindful communication, setting aside time each week to check in with each other without distractions. They listen fully, without interrupting or jumping to conclusions. Over time, this practice deepens their connection and reduces misunderstandings.
- **Reflection**: Reflect on a relationship in your life that could benefit from mindful communication. How can you bring more presence, patience, and empathy to your interactions with this person?

6.3 Enhanced Well-Being

Over time, mindfulness helps cultivate a deep sense of well-being, grounded in acceptance and presence. Instead of constantly striving for the next achievement or worrying about the future, mindfulness teaches us to appreciate the present moment, leading to greater contentment and inner peace.

Quote from Thich Nhat Hanh:
"The present moment is filled with joy and happiness. If you are attentive, you will see it."
This quote reminds us that joy and peace are available to us in every moment—we simply need to be present enough to notice them.

Conclusion to Chapter 2: The Journey of Mindfulness

Mindfulness is a lifelong practice that offers both immediate and long-term rewards. It's a way of being in the world that allows you to let go of unnecessary stress, cultivate presence, and create space for peace and clarity.

As you continue your mindfulness journey, remember that each moment offers an opportunity to practice. Whether you're meditating, working, or simply breathing, mindfulness invites you to show up fully for your life. In the next chapter, we'll explore how letting go of perfectionism—often one of the greatest obstacles to inner peace—can help you embrace self-compassion, authenticity, and freedom.

Chapter 3: Letting Go of Perfectionism

Introduction to Letting Go of Perfectionism

Perfectionism is often seen as a badge of honor. We believe that striving for perfection will make us more successful, respected, or admired. In reality, perfectionism can be a heavy burden—one that creates anxiety, stress, and a perpetual sense of inadequacy. It keeps us trapped in a cycle of self-criticism, as we set impossibly high standards and then berate ourselves when we inevitably fall short.

Letting go of perfectionism is about embracing our inherent worthiness, regardless of our achievements or mistakes. It's about accepting ourselves as we are—imperfect and human. In this chapter, we will explore the roots of perfectionism, the toll it takes on our mental and emotional well-being, and practical strategies for letting go of the need to be perfect. We'll also delve into the practice of self-compassion, a powerful antidote to perfectionism.

Section 1: Understanding the Roots of Perfectionism

Perfectionism doesn't appear out of nowhere—it's usually rooted in deeper beliefs about ourselves and our value. For many, perfectionism starts in childhood, when approval and love might have felt conditional upon success or good behavior. Perhaps you were praised for achieving high grades or excelling in extracurricular activities, and from a young age, you internalized the message that your worth is tied to your accomplishments.

1.1 The Fear of Failure

At the heart of perfectionism is a deep fear of failure. Perfectionists often believe that making mistakes will lead to judgment, criticism, or rejection. This fear can become so intense that it paralyzes us, making us avoid risks and challenges that might expose our imperfections. We become so focused on avoiding failure that we lose sight of the opportunities for growth and learning that come from embracing imperfection.

1.2 The Desire for Approval

Perfectionism is also driven by a desire for approval and validation. Many perfectionists are people-pleasers who believe that if they can just be "good enough" or "perfect enough," they will earn the love, respect, or admiration of others. This constant pursuit of external validation can lead to burnout and emotional exhaustion, as we feel the pressure to live up to expectations that may be unrealistic or impossible.

1.3 Cultural and Societal Pressures

In today's world, cultural and societal pressures fuel perfectionism. Social media, in particular, presents a curated and idealized version of other people's lives, making it easy to fall into the trap of comparison. We see influencers and celebrities with seemingly flawless lives, and we start to believe that we must match this level of perfection in our own lives. This creates a toxic cycle of comparison and inadequacy.

Section 2: The Costs of Perfectionism

Perfectionism may seem like a virtue, but it comes at a significant cost. While striving for excellence can be healthy, perfectionism takes it to an unhealthy extreme, often leading to stress, anxiety, and burnout.

2.1 Emotional and Mental Costs

Perfectionism often leads to a harsh inner critic. When we don't meet our impossibly high standards, we engage in negative self-talk, telling ourselves we're not good enough, smart enough, or talented enough. This inner dialogue erodes our self-esteem and makes it difficult to experience joy or satisfaction, even when we succeed.

Case Study:

Consider the story of Maya, a high-achieving professional who constantly strives for perfection in her career. Despite her many successes, Maya often feels like a failure because she fixates on minor mistakes or areas where she could have done better. This chronic self-criticism has led to anxiety, sleepless nights, and an inability to enjoy her accomplishments. Maya's story is not unique—many perfectionists experience similar emotional turmoil as they chase an unattainable ideal.

2.2 Physical Costs

The stress of perfectionism can also take a physical toll. Studies have shown that people with perfectionist tendencies are more prone to stress-related illnesses, including headaches, digestive problems, and heart disease. The constant pressure to perform perfectly can trigger chronic stress, leading to increased levels of cortisol, the body's stress hormone. Over time, this can weaken the immune system and increase the risk of burnout.

2.3 Impact on Relationships

Perfectionism doesn't just affect our relationship with ourselves—it can also strain our relationships with others. Perfectionists often project their high standards onto the people around them, leading to unrealistic expectations in friendships, romantic relationships, and even parenting. This can create tension, disappointment, and resentment when others inevitably fail to live up to these expectations.

Section 3: Embracing Imperfection

The first step in letting go of perfectionism is embracing the idea that imperfection is not only inevitable but also essential to growth and learning. By accepting our imperfections, we allow ourselves the freedom to make mistakes, learn from them, and move forward without the weight of self-judgment.

3.1 The Beauty of Imperfection

In Japanese culture, there is a concept known as **wabi-sabi**, which celebrates the beauty of imperfection. Wabi-sabi teaches us to find beauty in flaws, incompleteness, and impermanence. This philosophy can be a powerful tool for perfectionists, as it encourages us to let go of the need for everything to be perfect and instead appreciate things as they are.

Exercise: The Imperfection Challenge
- **Instructions**: For the next week, challenge yourself to do one thing imperfectly each day. This could be something small, like leaving a typo in an email, or something bigger, like trying a new hobby without worrying about being good at it. As you complete each task, reflect on how it felt to let go of the need for perfection. Did it feel uncomfortable? Liberating? How did others respond to your imperfection?

3.2 Redefining Success

Letting go of perfectionism requires redefining what success means to you. Instead of measuring success by external outcomes—such as flawless performance or meeting every expectation—consider success in terms of effort, growth, and learning. When we shift our focus from outcomes to the process, we can begin to appreciate the journey rather than fixating on the destination.

Exercise: Redefining Success
- **Instructions**: Take some time to reflect on your current definition of success. How do you measure success in your personal life, career, and relationships? Now, write down a new definition of success that focuses on growth, effort, and authenticity rather than perfection. For example, "Success means showing up and giving my best effort, even if the outcome isn't perfect," or "Success is learning from my mistakes and growing in the process." Keep this new definition of success somewhere visible, and refer to it whenever you feel the pressure of perfectionism creeping in.

3.3 Practicing Self-Compassion

Self-compassion is the most powerful antidote to perfectionism. **Dr. Kristin Neff**, a leading researcher in self-compassion, explains that when we practice self-compassion, we treat ourselves with the same kindness and understanding that we would offer a close friend. Instead of beating ourselves up for our mistakes or shortcomings, we acknowledge that we are human and that everyone makes mistakes.

Self-compassion involves three key elements:
- **Self-kindness**: Treating yourself with warmth and understanding, rather than criticism.
- **Common humanity**: Recognizing that everyone struggles and makes mistakes—it's part of being human.
- **Mindfulness**: Being present with your emotions without becoming overwhelmed by them.

Exercise: The Self-Compassion Break
- **Instructions**: The next time you find yourself being self-critical, pause and take a self-compassion break. Start by acknowledging the difficulty of the moment: "This is a moment of suffering." Then, remind yourself that suffering is part of the human experience: "Everyone struggles; I'm not alone." Finally, offer yourself kindness: "May I be kind to myself in this moment." Repeat these phrases as needed, allowing yourself to soften in the face of self-criticism.

Section 4: Letting Go of the Need for External Validation

Perfectionists often seek external validation—whether it's praise from a boss, approval from a partner, or likes on social media. But relying on external validation for your sense of self-worth is a never-ending cycle. No matter how much approval you receive, it will never feel like enough because you are seeking validation outside of yourself.

4.1 Shifting from External to Internal Validation

The key to breaking free from the need for external validation is learning to validate yourself. This means cultivating an inner sense of worth that is not dependent on others' opinions or approval. It's about knowing that you are enough just as you are, regardless of what others think.

Exercise: Self-Validation Practice
- **Instructions**: Each day, take a few moments to reflect on something you did well, regardless of whether or not it was acknowledged by others. This could be a small achievement, like sticking to a morning routine, or a larger one, like completing a project at work. Write it down and affirm yourself: "I'm proud of myself for doing this, even if no one else noticed." Over time, this practice will help you build a stronger sense of internal validation.

4.2 Letting Go of Comparison

Comparison is one of the greatest barriers to letting go of perfectionism. When we compare ourselves to others, we often focus on their successes and highlight our perceived shortcomings. This leads to a sense of inadequacy and fuels the belief that we must be perfect in order to be worthy.

Quote from Theodore Roosevelt:
"Comparison is the thief of joy." This quote reminds us that when we compare ourselves to others, we rob ourselves of the happiness and satisfaction that comes from appreciating our own unique journey.

Exercise: The Social Media Detox
- **Instructions**: For one week, commit to a social media detox. During this time, avoid platforms that encourage comparison, like Instagram or Facebook. Instead, focus on activities that bring you joy, fulfillment, and connection in the real world. After the week is over, reflect on how stepping away from social media impacted your self-perception and mood. Did it help you let go of comparison and the

need to be perfect?

Section 5: The Courage to Be Vulnerable

Letting go of perfectionism requires vulnerability. It means being willing to show up as your authentic self, flaws and all. Vulnerability is not a weakness—it's a strength. **Brené Brown**, one of the leading researchers on vulnerability and shame, explains that vulnerability is at the core of meaningful human experiences, such as love, belonging, and joy. But vulnerability also exposes us to the possibility of criticism, rejection, and failure—things that perfectionists often try to avoid at all costs.

However, to let go of perfectionism, we must be willing to embrace vulnerability. This means showing up as our authentic selves, even when it feels uncomfortable or risky. It means accepting that we are enough, even when we're not perfect, and allowing others to see us in our raw, unfiltered state.

5.1 The Connection Between Perfectionism and Shame

At the root of perfectionism is often a deep-seated sense of shame. Shame tells us that we are not enough—that we need to be perfect in order to be loved or accepted. Perfectionism, then, becomes a way of protecting ourselves from this fear of shame. If we can just do everything perfectly, we think, we can avoid feelings of unworthiness.

Brené Brown describes shame as the fear of disconnection—the belief that if others see our flaws and vulnerabilities, they will reject us. Perfectionism is a response to this fear, as it pushes us to hide our imperfections and strive for unattainable standards.

5.2 Vulnerability as a Path to Connection

The paradox of perfectionism is that while we use it to protect ourselves from rejection, it actually creates disconnection. When we try to appear perfect, we put up walls between ourselves and others. We hide our true selves, fearing that we will be judged or criticized if we reveal our imperfections. But the reality is that vulnerability is what fosters genuine connection.

When we allow ourselves to be vulnerable—to admit our mistakes, share our struggles, and be open about our imperfections—we give others permission to do the same. Vulnerability invites empathy and compassion, both from ourselves and from others. It allows us to connect on a deeper level, where real trust and intimacy can grow.

Exercise: Practicing Vulnerability
- **Instructions**: Think of a situation where you've been hiding your vulnerability out of fear of judgment or rejection. It could be at work, in a relationship, or even with friends. Choose a small step toward vulnerability—perhaps sharing a mistake, expressing an insecurity, or asking for help. Reflect on how it feels to show up authentically in this situation, without the need to be perfect.
- **Reflection**: After practicing vulnerability, reflect on how the experience affected your sense of connection with others. Did showing vulnerability strengthen your relationships or invite more empathy? How did it feel to release the need for perfection and embrace your true self?

5.3 The Strength in Embracing Imperfection

Vulnerability is not about exposing ourselves recklessly—it's about having the courage to show up as we are, even when we fear that we might not be enough. It's about accepting that imperfection is a part of life and that we are still worthy of love, belonging, and connection, even when we make mistakes.

In **Daring Greatly**, **Brené Brown** talks about how embracing vulnerability allows us to live wholeheartedly. When we let go of perfectionism, we allow ourselves to experience life more fully. We stop holding back out of fear of failure or judgment and instead open ourselves up to the possibility of joy, love, and connection.

Quote from Brené Brown:
"Vulnerability sounds like truth and feels like courage. Truth and courage aren't always comfortable, but they're never weakness." This quote reminds us that while vulnerability may feel uncomfortable, it is also the source of true strength.

Section 6: Perfectionism in Relationships

Perfectionism doesn't just affect our relationship with ourselves—it also impacts how we relate to others. In relationships, perfectionism can manifest as unrealistic expectations, controlling behavior, or the fear of vulnerability. It can lead to dissatisfaction and conflict, as we expect ourselves and others to live up to impossible standards.

6.1 Unrealistic Expectations in Relationships

Perfectionists often project their high standards onto others, expecting them to be flawless as well. This can create strain in relationships, as partners, friends, or family members feel pressured to meet unrealistic expectations. When others fall short of these expectations (as they inevitably will), it can lead to frustration, disappointment, and even resentment.

For example, if you expect your partner to always know exactly what you need without having to communicate it, you're setting them up for failure. If you expect your friends to always be available when you need them, you're bound to feel disappointed when they have their own lives to attend to.

Letting go of perfectionism in relationships means releasing the need for others to be perfect. It means accepting that everyone has flaws, and that relationships are about connection, not perfection.

Exercise: Identifying Unrealistic Expectations
- **Instructions**: Reflect on your relationships—whether with a partner, friend, or family member. Write down any expectations you have of them that might be unrealistic or perfectionistic. For example, do you expect them to always agree with you, never make mistakes, or always meet your needs? Next, reflect on how these expectations affect your relationship. Are they causing frustration or tension?
- **Reflection**: After identifying these expectations, think about how you can let go of them. How can you accept your loved ones as they are, rather than expecting them to be perfect? How might releasing these expectations improve your relationships and create more space for empathy and understanding?

6.2 Letting Go of Control in Relationships

Perfectionism in relationships often shows up as a need for control. We may try to control how our loved ones behave, how they respond to us, or how they show up in the relationship. This need for control can create tension, as it leaves little room for spontaneity, authenticity, or compromise.

Letting go of control in relationships means trusting that others are capable of making their own decisions, even if they don't always align with what we want. It means allowing others to be themselves, rather than trying to mold them into an idealized version of who we think they should be.

Exercise: Releasing the Need for Control

- **Instructions**: Think about a situation in your relationship where you've tried to control the outcome. For example, have you tried to control how your partner handles a disagreement, or how your friend responds to a situation? Reflect on how this need for control has affected the relationship. Next, write down one action you can take to release control in this area—whether it's stepping back, letting go of expectations, or allowing the other person to make their own decisions.
- **Reflection**: After taking this step, reflect on how it felt to let go of control. Did it create more space for understanding or connection in the relationship? How can you continue practicing this in other areas of your relationships?

6.3 Practicing Vulnerability in Relationships

As discussed earlier, vulnerability is essential for deepening connection in relationships. When we let go of the need to appear perfect, we allow ourselves to be seen for who we truly are. This opens the door to deeper intimacy, trust, and understanding.

Exercise: Sharing Your Imperfections
- **Instructions**: Choose a relationship where you feel comfortable practicing vulnerability. Share something with the other person that you've been holding back—whether it's a fear, an insecurity, or a mistake you've made. Notice how the other person responds. Did they offer empathy or understanding? How did being vulnerable impact your connection with them?
- **Reflection**: Reflect on how showing your imperfections in this relationship affected your sense of connection. Did it create more openness or trust? How can you continue practicing vulnerability in this and other relationships?

Section 7: Perfectionism in the Workplace

Perfectionism often shows up in the workplace, where we feel the pressure to perform at our best, meet deadlines, and exceed expectations. While striving for excellence can be a positive trait, perfectionism takes it to an unhealthy extreme, leading to burnout, anxiety, and a constant fear of failure.

7.1 The Perfectionism-Productivity Trap

One of the ways perfectionism manifests in the workplace is through the belief that we must always be productive and efficient. Perfectionists often push themselves to work longer hours, take on more responsibilities, and avoid asking for help, fearing that doing less would reflect poorly on their competence or worth.

However, this perfectionism-productivity trap can backfire. Working longer hours doesn't necessarily mean working better, and the constant pressure to be perfect can lead to burnout and decreased performance over time.

Exercise: Challenging the Perfectionism-Productivity Myth

- **Instructions**: Take some time to reflect on your relationship with productivity at work. Do you equate your worth with how much you accomplish? Do you feel guilty when you take breaks or when things don't go perfectly? Write down one or two areas where you've noticed perfectionism affecting your work habits—such as working late hours, avoiding delegation, or not taking time off. Then, commit to setting a boundary in one of these areas. For example, you might set a limit on how late you stay at work or delegate a task that you've been holding onto out of fear of imperfection.
- **Reflection**: After setting this boundary, reflect on how it impacted your workday. Did you feel less stressed or more balanced? How can letting go of perfectionism at work enhance your productivity and well-being?

7.2 Embracing Mistakes as Opportunities for Growth

In the workplace, perfectionists often see mistakes as catastrophic events. A small error can feel like a personal failure, leading to self-doubt and anxiety. This mindset causes many perfectionists to avoid risks or new opportunities, for fear that they won't meet their high standards. But mistakes are not failures—they are essential steps in the learning process.

In fact, **Carol Dweck**, the psychologist who pioneered the concept of the growth mindset, argues that people who embrace mistakes as learning opportunities are more likely to achieve long-term success. When we let go of the idea that we need to be perfect, we open ourselves to experimentation, innovation, and growth.

Case Study:

Imagine a project manager named Alex, who avoids taking on challenging projects because they fear making mistakes. They believe that if they don't perform perfectly, they will disappoint their team or lose their credibility.

However, after attending a leadership workshop that encourages a growth mindset, Alex decides to take on a high-risk project. Along the way, they make several mistakes, but instead of hiding or feeling ashamed, Alex uses the feedback from their team to improve the project. By the end, the project is a success—not because Alex avoided mistakes, but because they learned and adapted along the way.

Exercise: Reframing Mistakes as Growth Opportunities
- **Instructions**: Think of a recent mistake or challenge you faced at work. Instead of focusing on what went wrong, write down three things you learned from the experience. How did this mistake help you grow or improve? What new skills or insights did you gain? Next, reflect on how you can use this experience to approach future challenges with more confidence and openness to growth.
- **Reflection**: After completing this exercise, reflect on how it feels to shift your perspective from failure to growth. Does it make you feel more empowered to take risks and try new things at work? How can this mindset shift help you let go of perfectionism in your professional life?

7.3 Letting Go of People-Pleasing in the Workplace

Another manifestation of perfectionism at work is people-pleasing. Many perfectionists feel the need to constantly meet the expectations of their boss, colleagues, or clients, even if it means sacrificing their own needs or boundaries. This can lead to overcommitment, burnout, and resentment, as they try to be everything to everyone.

Letting go of people-pleasing doesn't mean becoming selfish or neglecting your responsibilities—it means setting healthy boundaries and recognizing that you can't make everyone happy all the time. When you let go of the need to be liked or approved of by everyone, you free yourself from the pressure to be perfect and allow yourself to focus on what truly matters.

Exercise: Setting Boundaries at Work
- **Instructions**: Identify an area at work where you've been engaging in people-pleasing behavior. Perhaps you've been taking on extra tasks that aren't part of your role, or you've been avoiding saying "no" to requests that are beyond your capacity. Write down one specific boundary you can set in this area. For example, you might decide to say "no" to taking on a new project or ask for more time to complete an existing one.

- **Reflection**: After setting this boundary, reflect on how it felt to assert yourself and protect your time and energy. Did it feel uncomfortable at first? How did others respond? How can setting boundaries help you let go of people-pleasing and perfectionism at work?

7.4 Redefining Success in the Workplace

Just as we need to redefine success in our personal lives, we also need to rethink what success looks like in the workplace. Many perfectionists equate success with flawless performance, constant productivity, and receiving praise or recognition from others. But true success is not about perfection—it's about growth, contribution, and balance.

Exercise: Defining Success on Your Own Terms
- **Instructions**: Take some time to reflect on your current definition of success at work. How do you measure your success? Is it based on external validation (e.g., promotions, praise, meeting deadlines perfectly), or is it based on your own values and growth? Write down a new definition of success that aligns with your authentic values. For example, "Success means contributing to meaningful work and growing through challenges, even when things don't go perfectly," or "Success is maintaining a balance between my career and personal well-being."
- **Reflection**: How does this new definition of success change the way you approach your work? Does it help you let go of perfectionism and feel more at peace with the process? How can this shift in mindset improve your overall work-life balance and job satisfaction?

Section 8: Perfectionism and Self-Care

One of the greatest challenges perfectionists face is making time for self-care. Many perfectionists believe that they must be constantly productive, always striving for more, and they feel guilty when they take time for themselves. But neglecting self-care leads to burnout, stress, and diminished well-being.

Letting go of perfectionism requires us to prioritize self-care, recognizing that rest and rejuvenation are not indulgent—they are essential. When we take care of ourselves, we are better able to show up fully in all areas of our lives, including our work, relationships, and personal growth.

8.1 The Importance of Rest and Recovery

Rest is often undervalued in a culture that celebrates busyness and hustle. But the truth is, our minds and bodies need regular periods of rest in order to function optimally. When we neglect rest, we become more prone to mistakes, stress, and emotional exhaustion. Letting go of perfectionism means acknowledging that we don't have to be "on" all the time. We are allowed to rest.

Exercise: Scheduling Rest
- **Instructions**: Take out your calendar and schedule at least one hour of rest or relaxation each day for the next week. This could be time spent reading, taking a walk, meditating, or simply doing nothing. Treat this time as non-negotiable, just like you would a work meeting or appointment. After each day's rest period, reflect on how it impacted your mood, energy levels, and overall well-being.
- **Reflection**: After completing a week of scheduled rest, reflect on how it felt to prioritize your well-being. Did it help you feel more balanced, energized, or relaxed? How can you continue to make rest and self-care a regular part of your routine, without feeling guilty or unproductive?

8.2 Letting Go of "All or Nothing" Thinking

Perfectionists often engage in "all or nothing" thinking, which can sabotage their self-care efforts. For example, if they can't fit in a full workout, they might skip exercise altogether. Or if they slip up on their diet, they might abandon their healthy eating habits entirely. This rigid thinking makes it difficult to practice self-care consistently, as perfectionists feel that if they can't do something perfectly, it's not worth doing at all.

Letting go of "all or nothing" thinking means embracing flexibility and progress over perfection. It's about recognizing that small efforts add up over time, and that taking care of yourself doesn't have to be perfect to be effective.

Exercise: Practicing Flexibility in Self-Care
- **Instructions**: Identify an area of your self-care routine where you've been engaging in "all or nothing" thinking. For example, maybe you've been avoiding exercise because you don't have time for a full workout, or you've been skipping meals because you're too busy to prepare something healthy. Write down one small, flexible step you can take to practice self-care, even if it's not perfect. For example, you might commit to a 10-minute walk instead of a full workout, or make a quick smoothie instead of skipping lunch.

- **Reflection**: After practicing flexibility in your self-care routine, reflect on how it felt to let go of "all or nothing" thinking. Did it help you feel more empowered to take care of yourself, even in small ways? How can you continue to embrace flexibility and consistency over perfection in your self-care practices?

Section 9: Moving Forward with Self-Compassion

As we conclude this chapter, it's important to remember that letting go of perfectionism is not something that happens overnight. It's a gradual process that requires patience, practice, and a commitment to self-compassion. There will be moments when perfectionism rears its head—when you feel the pressure to be perfect or the fear of failure starts to creep in. In these moments, remember to be kind to yourself.

9.1 Self-Compassion as a Daily Practice

Self-compassion is not just something you practice when things go wrong—it's a daily habit that helps you navigate life's ups and downs with grace and kindness. By cultivating self-compassion, you build resilience, reduce stress, and learn to accept yourself as you are, imperfections and all.

Exercise: Daily Self-Compassion Practice
- **Instructions**: Each morning, take a few minutes to practice self-compassion. Begin by placing your hand on your heart and taking a few deep breaths. Then, repeat the following phrases (or create your own): "May I be kind to myself today. May I accept myself as I am. May I remember that I am worthy of love and respect, even when I make mistakes." Throughout the day, whenever you notice self-critical thoughts arising, gently return to these affirmations.
- **Reflection**: After a week of practicing daily self-compassion, reflect on how this practice has impacted your mindset and emotional well-being. Did you notice a shift in the way you spoke to yourself during challenging moments? How did treating yourself with kindness and understanding affect your mood and stress levels? Moving forward, consider how you can make self-compassion an ongoing part of your daily routine, especially when perfectionism and self-criticism arise.

Section 9.2: Embracing the Journey Over the Destination

Letting go of perfectionism is not about abandoning high standards or the desire to achieve excellence. It's about recognizing that the journey is more important than the destination. When we become so fixated on achieving a perfect outcome, we lose sight of the growth, learning, and joy that come from simply being present with the process.

Perfectionists often delay happiness, thinking they will only be worthy of joy or fulfillment once they have achieved a certain goal. But true fulfillment comes from embracing the messy, imperfect process of growth and discovery. By letting go of the need for perfect outcomes, you free yourself to live more fully in the present moment.

Exercise: Celebrating Progress, Not Perfection
- **Instructions**: At the end of each week, set aside time to reflect on your progress in any area of your life—whether it's work, personal growth, relationships, or self-care. Instead of focusing on what you didn't achieve or where you fell short, celebrate the small steps you took toward growth. Write down three things you're proud of from the week, no matter how small. It could be completing a task, learning from a mistake, or practicing self-compassion.
- **Reflection**: How does celebrating your progress, rather than striving for perfection, change the way you feel about yourself? Does it help you feel more fulfilled and at peace with where you are? How can you continue to shift your focus from the destination to the journey in your everyday life?

Section 9.3: Cultivating a Growth Mindset

One of the most powerful ways to let go of perfectionism is by cultivating a growth mindset—a concept developed by psychologist **Carol Dweck**. A growth mindset is the belief that our abilities and intelligence can be developed through effort, learning, and perseverance. In contrast, a fixed mindset—the belief that our talents are static—fuels perfectionism because it makes us fear failure and avoid challenges.

When you adopt a growth mindset, you no longer see mistakes as failures or signs of inadequacy. Instead, you see them as opportunities to grow and improve. This mindset shift helps you embrace imperfection as part of the learning process, making it easier to let go of perfectionism and embrace continuous growth.

Exercise: Shifting to a Growth Mindset
- **Instructions**: Think of an area in your life where you've been afraid

to take risks or try new things due to fear of failure or perfectionism. Now, imagine how you might approach this area with a growth mindset. Write down one or two ways you can start viewing challenges or setbacks as opportunities to learn, rather than as threats to your self-worth. For example, instead of saying, "I'm not good at this," try reframing it as, "I'm still learning, and I'll improve with practice."

- **Reflection**: After practicing this shift in mindset, reflect on how it impacted your approach to challenges. Did you feel more willing to take risks or try new things? How can adopting a growth mindset help you let go of perfectionism and embrace a more flexible, resilient approach to life?

Conclusion to Chapter 3: Freedom in Letting Go of Perfectionism
Letting go of perfectionism is an act of liberation. It frees you from the impossible standards you've set for yourself and opens the door to self-compassion, growth, and authentic connection. When you let go of the need to be perfect, you give yourself permission to be human—to make mistakes, to learn, to grow, and to show up as your true self.

Perfectionism may be a difficult habit to break, but as you've seen in this chapter, there are practical steps you can take to release its grip. From practicing vulnerability and self-compassion to embracing a growth mindset, each small step you take toward letting go of perfectionism brings you closer to living a life of greater peace, joy, and fulfillment.

Remember, letting go of perfectionism is not about giving up on your goals or lowering your standards. It's about embracing the beauty of imperfection and allowing yourself to experience the full range of human emotions, challenges, and triumphs. It's about realizing that you are enough, just as you are.

As we move into the next chapter, we'll explore how creating space in your life—both physically and mentally—can help you let go of what no longer serves you and make room for what truly matters. By simplifying your environment, your schedule, and your mind, you'll create the freedom and clarity needed to live with greater intention and peace.

Chapter 4: Creating Space for Yourself

Introduction to Creating Space

In a world filled with endless distractions, responsibilities, and noise, it can feel as though we are constantly operating at maximum capacity. Our minds are cluttered with worries and to-do lists, our schedules are packed with commitments, and our physical spaces are overflowing with possessions. All of this can leave us feeling overwhelmed, stressed, and disconnected from ourselves.

Creating space for yourself—physically, mentally, and emotionally—is essential for letting go of what no longer serves you and making room for what truly matters. In this chapter, we will explore the power of decluttering, not only your environment but also your mind and your life. By clearing out the unnecessary, you'll create space for clarity, peace, and intention.

Section 1: The Importance of Space
Before diving into the practical steps for creating space, it's important to understand why space—whether physical, mental, or emotional—is so essential to our well-being.

1.1 The Connection Between Clutter and Stress

Research shows that clutter has a direct impact on our stress levels. Studies from **Dr. Sherrie Bourg Carter**, a psychologist specializing in stress management, indicate that a cluttered environment leads to feelings of overwhelm, anxiety, and frustration. When our physical surroundings are chaotic, it's difficult for our minds to relax and focus. We are constantly reminded of unfinished tasks, disorganization, and the weight of things we haven't dealt with.

Just as physical clutter creates mental chaos, a cluttered mind can make it difficult to prioritize, make decisions, and find peace. Without space, we feel pulled in a thousand different directions, unable to fully engage with any one thing.

Quote from Marie Kondo:
"The best way to find out what we really need is to get rid of what we don't." This philosophy is at the heart of decluttering—not just your physical space, but also your mental and emotional space. When we let go of the excess, we

create room for clarity, focus, and joy.

1.2 Space as a Catalyst for Personal Growth

When we make space in our lives—whether by simplifying our environment, freeing up time in our schedules, or clearing out mental clutter—we create the conditions for personal growth. Space allows us to breathe, reflect, and be present. It gives us the freedom to explore new opportunities, connect with our inner selves, and cultivate deeper relationships with others.

Without space, we remain stuck in a cycle of busyness, stress, and distraction. But when we intentionally create space, we open the door to creativity, insight, and transformation.

Exercise: Reflecting on Your Need for Space

- **Instructions**: Take a moment to reflect on the current state of your life. Is your environment cluttered or disorganized? Is your schedule filled to the brim with commitments? Do you often feel mentally overwhelmed by tasks, worries, or distractions? Write down three areas of your life where you feel you need more space—physically, mentally, or emotionally. Next, write down how creating space in these areas might positively impact your well-being.
- **Reflection**: How does the idea of creating space make you feel? Does it bring a sense of relief or clarity? How can making space for yourself improve your ability to focus, relax, and enjoy life?

Section 2: Decluttering Your Physical Space

Your physical environment has a profound effect on your mental and emotional well-being. A cluttered space can leave you feeling scattered and stressed, while a clean, organized space can create a sense of calm and order. In this section, we will explore practical strategies for decluttering your home, workspace, and personal possessions, allowing you to create a peaceful environment that supports your well-being.

2.1 The Minimalist Mindset

Minimalism isn't just about owning fewer things—it's about living with intention. When you adopt a minimalist mindset, you become more selective about what you bring into your space and your life. You ask yourself, "Does this add value to my life?" If the answer is no, it may be time to let it go.

Marie Kondo's KonMari Method encourages us to keep only the items that "spark joy"—the things that genuinely add happiness, comfort, or purpose to our lives. Everything else is clutter that takes up space, both physically and mentally.

Exercise: The KonMari Decluttering Process
- **Instructions**: Choose one area of your home—such as a closet, a room, or even just a drawer—to begin decluttering. Go through each item, one by one, and ask yourself, "Does this item bring me joy or serve a necessary purpose in my life?" If the answer is yes, keep it. If the answer is no, thank the item for its service and let it go, either by donating, selling, or discarding it. Take your time with this process, focusing on one area at a time.
- **Reflection**: After decluttering a specific area, reflect on how the process made you feel. Did letting go of unnecessary possessions create a sense of relief or lightness? How does your environment feel now compared to before? How can you continue applying this minimalist mindset to other areas of your home and life?

2.2 Creating a Personal Sanctuary

Once you've decluttered your space, the next step is to create a personal sanctuary—a space in your home where you can relax, recharge, and practice mindfulness. Your sanctuary should be a place that feels peaceful and restorative, free from distractions and clutter. This space could be a corner of your living room, a reading nook, or even your bedroom.

Exercise: Designing Your Sanctuary
- **Instructions**: Choose a space in your home that you want to turn into a personal sanctuary. Start by clearing away any clutter or distractions. Then, think about what elements would make this space feel peaceful and inviting. You might want to add calming colors, soft lighting, comfortable seating, or items that bring you joy, such as plants, candles, or artwork. The goal is to create a space that feels like a retreat from the busyness of daily life.
- **Reflection**: After setting up your personal sanctuary, spend some time in the space. How does it feel to be in a space that is dedicated to rest and relaxation? How can you use this space as a regular retreat to practice mindfulness, meditate, or simply unwind?

2.3 Simplifying Your Digital Life

Physical clutter isn't the only thing that takes up space in our lives—our digital lives can become just as cluttered, with overflowing inboxes, endless notifications, and countless apps vying for our attention. Simplifying your digital life is just as important as decluttering your physical environment. By reducing digital distractions, you create mental space for focus, creativity, and connection.

Exercise: Digital Decluttering
- **Instructions**: Start by decluttering your digital devices. Go through your phone, computer, and tablet, and delete any apps, files, or photos that you no longer need. Organize your files into folders and unsubscribe from any email lists or notifications that add unnecessary noise to your inbox. Set aside specific times each day to check your email and social media, rather than constantly responding to notifications throughout the day.
- **Reflection**: After decluttering your digital life, reflect on how it feels to have fewer distractions. Did reducing digital clutter help you feel more focused or present? How can you continue simplifying your digital life moving forward?

Section 3: Creating Space in Your Schedule

Our schedules often feel as cluttered as our homes, filled with back-to-back commitments, obligations, and distractions. It's easy to fall into the trap of busyness, thinking that the more we do, the more productive or valuable we are. But a packed schedule can lead to burnout, stress, and a lack of time for the things that truly matter.

Creating space in your schedule means being intentional about how you spend your time. It's about prioritizing what's most important and letting go of the activities, obligations, or distractions that drain your energy.

3.1 The Myth of Busyness

In our culture, busyness is often equated with success. We wear our packed schedules like badges of honor, believing that the more we do, the more accomplished we are. But constant busyness is not a measure of success—it's a recipe for burnout.

Being busy all the time leaves little room for reflection, creativity, or connection. When we're constantly rushing from one task to the next, we miss out on the beauty of the present moment. Letting go of the need to be busy all the time allows us to slow down, focus on what truly matters, and live with greater intention.

Quote from Socrates:
"Beware the barrenness of a busy life." This quote serves as a reminder that busyness without purpose leads to emptiness. True fulfillment comes from being intentional with your time, rather than filling every moment with activity.

3.2 Prioritizing What Matters

One of the most important steps in creating space in your schedule is learning to prioritize. Not everything on your to-do list is equally important, and not every commitment deserves your time and energy. By focusing on what truly matters, you can free up time for the things that bring you joy, fulfillment, and peace.

Exercise: The Prioritization Matrix
- **Instructions**: Create a prioritization matrix by dividing a piece of paper into four quadrants:
    1. **Urgent and important**: Tasks that require immediate attention and have a significant impact.
    2. **Important but not urgent**: Tasks that are important for long-term goals but don't need immediate attention.
    3. **Urgent but not important**: Tasks that demand immediate attention but may not significantly impact your long-term goals or well-being (often interruptions or distractions).
    4. **Not urgent and not important**: Tasks that neither require immediate attention nor contribute to your well-being or long-term success (often time-wasters).

Once you've divided your tasks into these four categories, focus on completing the tasks in the **"urgent and important"** quadrant first. Then, make time for the **"important but not urgent"** tasks—these often represent your long-term goals, personal growth, or activities that bring you joy. Try to minimize the time you spend on tasks that fall into the **"urgent but not important"** and **"not urgent and not important"** quadrants.

Reflection: After organizing your tasks using the prioritization matrix, reflect on how it felt to focus on what truly matters. Did this exercise help you gain clarity about where to invest your time and energy? How can you continue applying this prioritization method to create more space in your schedule?

3.3 Learning to Say No

Many people struggle with saying "no" because they fear disappointing others or missing out on opportunities. However, constantly saying "yes" to every request or obligation leaves you with little time or energy for yourself.

Learning to say no is a powerful way to create space in your life for the things that truly matter.

When you say no to things that don't align with your priorities or values, you're not being selfish—you're honoring your time and energy. By setting boundaries, you create space for self-care, rest, and personal fulfillment.

Exercise: Practicing Saying No
- **Instructions**: Think of a recent situation where you felt obligated to say yes to something, even though you didn't want to. Reflect on why you said yes—was it out of guilt, fear of disappointing someone, or a desire to please others? Now, think about how saying yes affected your time, energy, or well-being. Going forward, practice saying no to at least one request or commitment each week that doesn't align with your values or priorities.
- **Reflection**: After practicing saying no, reflect on how it felt to set this boundary. Did it create more space for rest or activities that nourish you? How did others respond to your decision, and how can you continue practicing this skill in the future?

Section 4: Creating Mental Space

Creating space isn't just about decluttering your physical environment or schedule—it's also about making space in your mind. A cluttered mind, filled with worries, distractions, and mental noise, makes it difficult to focus, relax, or be present. By clearing out mental clutter, you create space for clarity, creativity, and peace.

4.1 Quieting the Mental Noise

Our minds are constantly racing with thoughts, worries, and mental to-do lists. This mental noise can make it difficult to focus, enjoy the present moment, or make clear decisions. One of the most effective ways to quiet the mental noise is through mindfulness and meditation.

When you practice mindfulness, you learn to observe your thoughts without attaching to them. This allows you to create space between your thoughts and your reactions, giving you more control over your mental state.

Exercise: Mindfulness Meditation for Mental Clarity
- **Instructions**: Set aside 10-15 minutes for a mindfulness meditation practice. Sit in a comfortable position, close your eyes, and focus on your breath. As thoughts arise, acknowledge them without judgment, and gently bring your focus back to your breath. The goal is not to stop your thoughts, but to create space between your thoughts and your awareness.
- **Reflection**: After your meditation, reflect on how it felt to create mental space. Did you notice a reduction in mental noise or a sense of clarity? How can you incorporate mindfulness into your daily routine to continue creating space in your mind?

4.2 Letting Go of Mental Clutter

Mental clutter often comes from holding onto worries, unresolved emotions, or tasks that are constantly weighing on your mind. Letting go of mental clutter requires acknowledging and processing these thoughts and feelings, rather than allowing them to take up space in your mind.

Exercise: The Mental Declutter Journal
- **Instructions**: Start a daily or weekly mental declutter journal. At the end of each day or week, take a few moments to write down anything that is weighing on your mind—whether it's worries, tasks, emotions, or distractions. The act of writing these things down helps externalize them, reducing their hold on your mind. Once they're written down, you can create an action plan for dealing with them or simply let them go.
- **Reflection**: After journaling, reflect on how it feels to release your thoughts and worries onto paper. Did it create more mental clarity or a sense of relief? How can this practice help you regularly clear out mental clutter and make space for peace and focus?

4.3 The Power of Single-Tasking

In today's fast-paced world, multitasking has become the norm. We try to juggle multiple tasks at once, believing that it will make us more productive. But research shows that multitasking actually decreases productivity and increases stress. Our brains are not wired to focus on multiple tasks at once, and switching between tasks causes mental fatigue.

Single-tasking—the practice of focusing on one task at a time—helps create mental space by allowing you to fully engage with what you're doing. It reduces overwhelm, improves focus, and increases the quality of your work.

Exercise: Practicing Single-Tasking
- **Instructions**: For the next week, practice single-tasking by focusing on one task at a time. Choose a task—whether it's answering emails, working on a project, or even eating a meal—and commit to focusing solely on that task until it's complete. Avoid checking your phone, switching tasks, or multitasking. If distractions arise, acknowledge them, but gently bring your focus back to the task at hand.
- **Reflection**: After practicing single-tasking for a week, reflect on how it affected your productivity and mental state. Did focusing on one task at a time help you feel more present or less overwhelmed? How can you continue to incorporate single-tasking into your daily routine to create more mental space?

Section 5: Creating Emotional Space

Creating emotional space means making room for your emotions without becoming overwhelmed by them. It involves acknowledging and processing your feelings, rather than pushing them aside or letting them build up over time. By creating emotional space, you can navigate life's challenges with greater clarity, balance, and resilience.

5.1 Allowing Yourself to Feel

Many people avoid or suppress their emotions because they fear being overwhelmed by them. But when we push our emotions aside, they don't disappear—they build up over time and eventually manifest as stress, anxiety, or even physical illness. Creating emotional space means allowing yourself to feel your emotions fully, without judgment or avoidance.

Exercise: Emotional Check-In
- **Instructions**: Set aside time each day for an emotional check-in. Sit quietly and take a few deep breaths. Then, ask yourself, "What am I feeling right now?" Allow yourself to name any emotions that come up—whether it's joy, sadness, frustration, or fear. Don't judge or try to change the emotions, simply observe them. If certain emotions feel overwhelming, place your hand on your heart and practice self-compassion, reminding yourself that it's okay to feel whatever you're feeling.
- **Reflection**: After your emotional check-in, reflect on how it felt to

create space for your emotions. Did acknowledging your feelings help you feel more grounded or at peace? How can this practice help you regularly process and release emotions, rather than letting them build up over time?

5.2 Setting Emotional Boundaries

Just as it's important to set boundaries in your schedule, it's also essential to set emotional boundaries with others. This means protecting your emotional energy by recognizing when you need to say no, take a break, or distance yourself from emotionally draining situations or people.

Exercise: Setting an Emotional Boundary
- **Instructions**: Reflect on a situation or relationship in your life where you've been giving more emotional energy than you can handle. Write down one specific boundary you can set to protect your emotional well-being. For example, you might decide to limit the time you spend with a particular person or set a boundary around how much emotional labor you're willing to take on in a situation.
- **Reflection**: After setting this emotional boundary, reflect on how it felt to protect your emotional energy. Did it create more space for self-care and emotional balance? How can you continue practicing emotional boundaries in other areas of your life?

Conclusion to Chapter 4: The Freedom of Creating Space

Creating space—physically, mentally, emotionally, and in your schedule—is one of the most powerful ways to let go of stress and overwhelm. By simplifying your environment, clearing your mind, and setting boundaries, you create the conditions for peace, clarity, and intentional living.

As you continue your journey of letting go, remember that creating space is an ongoing practice. Just as clutter builds up over time, so too does the need to regularly clear out what no longer serves you. Whether it's physical possessions, mental distractions, or emotional burdens, making space for yourself is an act of self-care and empowerment.

In the next chapter, we'll explore the transformative power of forgiveness and how letting go of past hurts can create space for healing, peace, and freedom.

Chapter 5: The Power of Forgiveness

Introduction to Forgiveness

Forgiveness is one of the most powerful tools we have for healing, yet it is also one of the most misunderstood. Many people view forgiveness as a sign of weakness, thinking that by forgiving someone, they are condoning harmful behavior or letting someone "off the hook." However, forgiveness is not about excusing wrongs or absolving others of responsibility—it is about freeing ourselves from the emotional burden of resentment and pain.

Holding onto grudges and past hurts weighs us down, affecting our mental, emotional, and even physical health. Forgiveness is an act of liberation. It allows us to let go of the pain caused by others and make space for healing, peace, and joy. This chapter will explore the power of forgiveness, why it is essential for personal well-being, and practical strategies for forgiving others—and ourselves.

Section 1: Understanding What Forgiveness Is (And What It Isn't)
Before diving into the process of forgiveness, it's important to clarify what forgiveness truly means, and just as importantly, what it doesn't mean. Forgiveness is often misunderstood, and these misconceptions can prevent people from embracing its healing power.

1.1 What Forgiveness *Isn't*

Forgiveness is often mistaken for weakness, passivity, or approval of bad behavior. However, none of these definitions truly capture the essence of forgiveness.

Forgiveness isn't:
- **Condoning**: Forgiveness does not mean that you are saying what someone did was okay. You are not absolving them of responsibility for their actions, nor are you forgetting the harm they caused.
- **Reconciliation**: Forgiving someone does not mean that you have to reconcile with them or continue a relationship with them. Forgiveness is something you do for yourself, independent of whether or not you maintain a connection with the person who hurt you.
- **A one-time event**: Forgiveness is often a process rather than a one-time decision. For deep wounds, forgiveness may take time, and it's

normal to revisit the process multiple times as you heal.

1.2 What Forgiveness *Is*

Forgiveness is a conscious choice to release resentment and anger, regardless of whether or not the other person "deserves" it. It is about freeing yourself from the toxic effects of holding onto hurt and bitterness. By forgiving, you are not condoning the wrongdoing—you are simply choosing to let go of its hold on your emotions and well-being.

Psychologist and author Dr. Fred Luskin, known for his work on forgiveness, explains that forgiveness is about reclaiming your personal power. When we refuse to forgive, we give the person who hurt us ongoing control over our emotional state. But when we forgive, we reclaim that power and choose peace over pain.

Exercise: Defining Forgiveness in Your Own Words
- **Instructions**: Take a few moments to reflect on what forgiveness means to you. Write down your own definition of forgiveness, based on your personal experiences. How does this definition align with the explanations provided above? Next, write down any misconceptions or fears you have about forgiveness, and how you can reframe those beliefs to make room for healing.
- **Reflection**: After completing this exercise, reflect on how your understanding of forgiveness has shifted. Did clarifying what forgiveness is (and isn't) help you feel more open to the idea of forgiving others? How can this new understanding guide you as you work toward forgiveness in your own life?

Section 2: The Emotional and Physical Burden of Holding onto Grudges

Holding onto anger, resentment, or bitterness doesn't just affect our emotional well-being—it also takes a significant toll on our physical health. When we hold onto grudges, our bodies remain in a heightened state of stress, which can lead to a variety of health issues over time.

2.1 The Emotional Cost of Holding onto Anger
Holding onto past hurts keeps us stuck in a cycle of anger and pain. Instead of moving forward, we replay the hurt over and over in our minds, which reinforces feelings of resentment and victimhood. This emotional weight can

prevent us from experiencing joy, love, or inner peace, as we are constantly consumed by thoughts of what was done to us.

Case Study: Consider the story of Rachel, who held a deep grudge against a former friend who betrayed her trust. For years, Rachel refused to forgive, feeling that doing so would mean excusing the betrayal. However, this choice kept Rachel locked in a state of bitterness. Every time she thought about the betrayal, she felt a surge of anger, which impacted her relationships with others and her ability to trust. When Rachel finally chose to forgive, it wasn't about excusing the betrayal—it was about freeing herself from the emotional chains that kept her stuck in the past.

2.2 The Physical Effects of Resentment

Research shows that chronic resentment and anger are linked to a variety of health problems, including high blood pressure, weakened immune function, and increased risk of heart disease. **Dr. Everett Worthington**, a leading researcher in the psychology of forgiveness, has found that individuals who practice forgiveness experience lower levels of stress and improved overall health.

When we hold onto anger, our bodies produce stress hormones such as cortisol and adrenaline. While these hormones are useful in short bursts (such as during a fight-or-flight response), chronic stress from prolonged anger or resentment can lead to inflammation, anxiety, and even depression.

Quote from Nelson Mandela:
"Resentment is like drinking poison and then hoping it will kill your enemies." This quote serves as a powerful reminder that holding onto anger doesn't harm the person who hurt you—it harms you.

Exercise: Reflecting on the Cost of Holding Grudges
- **Instructions**: Think of a specific grudge or resentment that you've been holding onto. Write down how this grudge has affected your emotional well-being. Has it caused you ongoing pain or stress? Has it impacted your relationships or your ability to trust others? Next, reflect on how holding onto this anger has affected your physical health. Have you experienced increased anxiety, sleeplessness, or other stress-related symptoms?
- **Reflection**: After completing this exercise, reflect on the emotional and physical toll of holding onto resentment. How might forgiving this person allow you to reclaim your peace and well-being? How does letting go of resentment benefit *you*, regardless of whether the

other person ever apologizes or changes?

Section 3: The Process of Forgiving Others

Forgiveness is not always easy, and it's certainly not something you can force yourself to do before you're ready. However, there are steps you can take to gradually work toward forgiveness, even for the deepest wounds.

3.1 Acknowledging the Hurt

The first step in forgiveness is acknowledging the pain that was caused. This may seem obvious, but many people avoid fully acknowledging their hurt out of fear that it will make them vulnerable or prolong their pain. However, healing begins with allowing yourself to feel and name the emotions associated with the hurt.

Exercise: Writing a Letter of Acknowledgment
- **Instructions**: Write a letter to the person who hurt you, acknowledging the pain they caused and how it has affected you. Be honest about your feelings, whether it's anger, sadness, betrayal, or disappointment. You don't have to send this letter—its purpose is to help you fully acknowledge and process the hurt. After writing the letter, read it over and reflect on how it feels to give voice to your pain.
- **Reflection**: How did acknowledging the hurt help you take the first step toward forgiveness? Did it allow you to release some of the emotional weight you've been carrying? How can accepting and naming your feelings be part of the healing process?

3.2 Practicing Empathy

One of the most powerful tools in forgiveness is empathy. This doesn't mean excusing someone's behavior, but rather, trying to understand the situation from their perspective. When we practice empathy, we acknowledge that people are often driven by their own pain, insecurities, or misunderstandings, and that their actions may not have been intended to harm us as deeply as they did.

Exercise: The Empathy Perspective Shift
- **Instructions**: Choose a person you are struggling to forgive and try to view the situation from their perspective. What might they have been feeling, fearing, or experiencing at the time? Were their actions driven by pain, confusion, or insecurity? Write down any insights that

come to mind as you try to understand their behavior. This doesn't mean you have to condone their actions, but it may help you soften your perspective and open the door to forgiveness.
- **Reflection**: Did practicing empathy help you view the situation with more understanding or compassion? How might this new perspective make it easier to let go of resentment and move toward forgiveness?

3.3 Letting Go of the Need for an Apology

One of the biggest barriers to forgiveness is the belief that the person who hurt us must apologize before we can forgive. While apologies can be meaningful, they are not always necessary for forgiveness. In fact, waiting for an apology may keep you stuck in a state of anger or bitterness, especially if the other person is unwilling or unable to apologize.

Forgiveness is something you do for yourself, regardless of whether the other person acknowledges their wrongdoing.

Exercise: Forgiving Without an Apology
- **Instructions**: Write down one step you can take to forgive this person, even without receiving an apology. This could involve letting go of your expectations for closure, mentally releasing the hold this person has over your emotions, or simply deciding that you are ready to free yourself from the resentment. After you've written this down, take a few moments to reflect on how forgiveness can benefit your peace of mind, even if the other person never acknowledges the hurt they caused.
- **Reflection**: How did letting go of the need for an apology affect your ability to move forward? Did it help you feel more empowered or in control of your emotional well-being? How can releasing the expectation for an apology help you find closure on your own terms?

3.4 Rituals for Forgiveness

Sometimes, forgiveness requires a symbolic gesture or ritual to help us process and release the hurt. Rituals can provide a sense of closure and give us the emotional space we need to move forward. Whether it's writing a letter, performing a symbolic act, or engaging in a personal ritual, these actions can help you consciously choose to let go.

Exercise: The Forgiveness Ritual
- **Instructions**: Choose a forgiveness ritual that resonates with you.

This could be writing a letter and then burning it, releasing balloons into the sky, or even performing a simple mindfulness meditation where you visualize yourself releasing the anger and pain. Whatever ritual you choose, make sure it feels meaningful and personal to you. After completing the ritual, take some time to sit quietly and reflect on the act of letting go.
- **Reflection**: How did performing a forgiveness ritual help you feel more at peace? Did it provide a sense of closure or relief? How can incorporating symbolic acts of forgiveness into your life help you heal from past hurts and release emotional burdens?

Section 4: Self-Forgiveness

While forgiving others is often difficult, self-forgiveness can be even harder. We are often our own harshest critics, holding onto guilt, shame, or regret long after the event has passed. Just as we must learn to forgive others for their mistakes, we must also learn to forgive ourselves for our own.

Self-forgiveness is about acknowledging our humanity and accepting that we are imperfect beings who sometimes make mistakes. It is about letting go of self-judgment and shame and embracing ourselves with compassion and understanding.

4.1 Acknowledging Your Mistakes

The first step in self-forgiveness is to acknowledge the mistakes or wrongs you've committed. This doesn't mean wallowing in guilt or shame, but rather, taking responsibility for your actions and reflecting on how they have affected others (and yourself). By acknowledging your mistakes without self-condemnation, you open the door to healing.

Exercise: The Self-Forgiveness Letter
- **Instructions**: Write a letter to yourself, acknowledging a mistake or wrong you've been holding onto. Be honest about how your actions impacted others or your own life, but approach yourself with kindness and compassion. Avoid self-blame or harsh criticism. After writing the letter, read it aloud to yourself, and then take a few deep breaths to release any lingering guilt or shame.
- **Reflection**: After writing the self-forgiveness letter, reflect on how it felt to acknowledge your mistake without self-judgment. Did it help you release some of the guilt or shame you've been carrying? How can practicing self-forgiveness allow you to move forward with

greater self-compassion and peace?

4.2 Releasing Self-Judgment

Self-forgiveness requires letting go of the harsh judgment and criticism we often direct toward ourselves. Many of us hold ourselves to impossibly high standards, and when we fall short, we punish ourselves with negative self-talk and feelings of unworthiness. But self-forgiveness is about accepting that mistakes are part of being human—and that we are still deserving of love, compassion, and kindness, even when we fall short.

Exercise: Challenging Negative Self-Talk
- **Instructions**: Pay attention to your inner dialogue for a day, particularly when you make a mistake or feel inadequate. When you notice negative self-talk—such as, "I'm not good enough" or "I always mess things up"—pause and challenge those thoughts. Replace them with more compassionate, realistic statements, such as, "I made a mistake, but I'm learning," or "I'm allowed to be imperfect." Write down a few of these compassionate statements and repeat them to yourself when self-judgment arises.
- **Reflection**: How did challenging your negative self-talk affect your emotional state? Did it help you feel more compassionate toward yourself? How can regularly practicing self-compassion and challenging self-judgment lead to greater emotional resilience and inner peace?

4.3 Learning from Your Mistakes

Forgiving yourself isn't just about letting go of guilt—it's also about learning from your mistakes and growing as a result. When you approach your mistakes with curiosity and openness, you can use them as opportunities for self-improvement and growth.

Exercise: Turning Mistakes into Lessons
- **Instructions**: Think of a mistake you've been holding onto—whether it's a personal failure, a decision you regret, or something that impacted your relationships or career. Instead of focusing on the guilt or shame you feel, reflect on what you've learned from the experience. Write down three lessons you've gained from this mistake and how it has contributed to your growth or personal development.
- **Reflection**: How did focusing on the lessons from your mistake shift your perspective? Did it help you release some of the guilt or regret? How can adopting a mindset of growth and learning help you

practice self-forgiveness more consistently?

Section 5: The Long-Term Benefits of Forgiveness

While forgiveness may feel challenging in the moment, the long-term benefits of practicing forgiveness—both toward others and yourself—are profound. By letting go of resentment, guilt, and anger, you create space for peace, emotional healing, and deeper connections with yourself and others.

5.1 Emotional Freedom

Forgiveness offers emotional freedom. When we forgive, we release ourselves from the heavy emotional burdens that come with holding onto past hurts or regrets. This emotional freedom allows us to live more fully in the present, rather than being weighed down by the pain of the past.

Case Study:

Consider the story of James, who spent years harboring anger toward his father for abandoning their family. This anger affected every aspect of James's life—his relationships, his career, and even his health. But when James chose to forgive his father, he experienced a profound sense of emotional freedom. Forgiveness didn't erase the pain of the past, but it allowed James to release the bitterness that was holding him back from living a fulfilling life.

5.2 Improved Relationships

Forgiveness can also improve your relationships with others. By letting go of grudges or past conflicts, you create space for empathy, understanding, and healing. Whether it's forgiving a partner, friend, or family member, forgiveness allows for deeper connection and trust, as it shows that you are willing to move forward, even when mistakes are made.

5.3 Healing and Peace

Ultimately, forgiveness brings healing and peace. It is a process of letting go of the emotional wounds that have been holding you back, allowing you to step into a future that is not defined by the pain of the past. Whether you are forgiving others or yourself, this process can be transformative, bringing a sense of inner peace and closure.

Conclusion to Chapter 5: The Freedom in Forgiveness

Forgiveness is a powerful act of self-liberation. By choosing to forgive—whether it's someone who has hurt you or yourself—you release the emotional burdens that have been weighing you down. Forgiveness is not about excusing wrongdoing or forgetting the past; it is about freeing yourself from the pain of holding onto resentment, guilt, or anger.

As you move forward on your journey of letting go, remember that forgiveness is a process, not a one-time event. It requires patience, self-compassion, and sometimes multiple attempts. But each step you take toward forgiveness brings you closer to emotional freedom, healing, and peace.

In the next chapter, we'll explore the importance of embracing change and how letting go of resistance to change can open up new possibilities for growth, happiness, and fulfillment. By learning to flow with life's inevitable transitions, you'll discover the freedom that comes from embracing the unknown.

Chapter 6: Embracing Change

Introduction to Embracing Change

Change is a constant in life. Whether we seek it or resist it, change is inevitable—relationships evolve, careers shift, loved ones pass away, and unexpected events disrupt our carefully laid plans. Yet, despite its inevitability, many of us struggle with change. We hold onto the familiar because it feels safe, even when it no longer serves us. The fear of the unknown often leads to resistance, which can manifest as anxiety, stress, or a sense of stagnation.

This chapter is about learning to embrace change rather than resisting it. By letting go of the need for certainty and control, you open yourself up to the possibilities that change can bring—new opportunities for growth, transformation, and happiness. Embracing change doesn't mean pretending that it's always easy or welcome, but rather learning to flow with life's natural rhythms and trusting in your ability to adapt and thrive.

Section 1: Why We Resist Change
To begin the process of embracing change, it's important to understand why we often resist it. Resistance to change is a natural human response, driven by a variety of fears and psychological factors. When we can identify the root causes of our resistance, we can begin to approach change with more openness and acceptance.

1.1 Fear of the Unknown

One of the primary reasons we resist change is fear of the unknown. As humans, we are wired to seek certainty and predictability because they provide a sense of safety. When faced with an uncertain future, our minds often conjure up worst-case scenarios, leading to anxiety and a desire to cling to what is familiar—even if the familiar is no longer working.

This fear of the unknown can prevent us from taking risks or embracing new opportunities. We might stay in a job that no longer fulfills us, remain in unhealthy relationships, or avoid pursuing our dreams because the potential for failure or discomfort feels too great. Yet, by holding onto the known, we limit ourselves and miss out on the growth and joy that come from stepping into the unknown.

Quote from Alan Watts:
"The only way to make sense out of change is to plunge into it, move with it, and join the dance." This quote reminds us that change, when embraced rather than feared, can be a dynamic and enriching part of life.

1.2 The Comfort of Routine

Routines provide structure and predictability, which is why many of us find comfort in them. However, while routines can be stabilizing, they can also become limiting if we rely on them to avoid change. When we become overly attached to our routines, we may resist opportunities for growth, adventure, or new experiences because they disrupt our established patterns.

Case Study:
Consider the story of John, a man who had been in the same job for 15 years. Despite feeling unfulfilled and burned out, he resisted looking for a new job because his routine gave him a sense of security. The idea of starting over in a new position felt daunting, and so he stayed in a role that made him increasingly unhappy. Eventually, after years of frustration, John took a leap of faith and accepted a job in a new field. The transition wasn't easy, but over time, he found that the change brought him a renewed sense of purpose and fulfillment.

1.3 Loss of Control

Change often triggers feelings of loss of control. When life changes—whether through a job loss, the end of a relationship, or an unexpected health crisis—we may feel as though the rug has been pulled out from under us. This sense of losing control can lead to resistance, as we try to cling to what we know in an attempt to regain stability.

However, it's important to recognize that control is often an illusion. We can't control every outcome in life, nor can we prevent unexpected changes from occurring. What we can control is how we respond to change. By shifting our focus from controlling external circumstances to managing our internal responses, we regain a sense of agency and resilience in the face of change.

Section 2: The Benefits of Embracing Change

While change can be uncomfortable and challenging, it also brings many benefits. When we learn to embrace change rather than resist it, we open ourselves up to personal growth, new opportunities, and a deeper sense of

fulfillment.
2.1 Personal Growth

Change is often the catalyst for personal growth. When we step outside our comfort zones and face new challenges, we develop new skills, insights, and strengths. Even when change feels difficult, it can lead to profound personal transformation.

Example:
Think of a time in your life when you faced a significant change, such as moving to a new city, starting a new job, or ending a relationship. At the time, the change may have felt overwhelming, but in hindsight, how did it contribute to your growth? Perhaps it taught you resilience, adaptability, or independence. Change often forces us to develop qualities we didn't know we had, helping us grow into more capable, confident versions of ourselves.

2.2 New Opportunities

Embracing change opens the door to new opportunities that would not be possible if we remained stuck in the status quo. Whether it's a career change, a new relationship, or a creative pursuit, change brings fresh possibilities that can enrich our lives in unexpected ways.

When we resist change, we close ourselves off to these opportunities, staying in situations that may feel safe but limit our potential. By letting go of fear and opening ourselves to change, we allow new doors to open, leading to experiences that can bring joy, fulfillment, and success.

Exercise: Identifying New Opportunities Through Change
- **Instructions**: Reflect on a change you are currently experiencing or a change you know is on the horizon. Write down any potential opportunities that this change could bring into your life. These opportunities might be personal growth, learning new skills, meeting new people, or even finding a new passion. Focus on the possibilities that change could open up, rather than the fear of what you might lose.
- **Reflection**: How does shifting your focus to the opportunities that change might bring affect your feelings about the change? Does it help you feel more open or optimistic? How can you continue to focus on the potential benefits of change, even when it feels challenging?

2.3 Increased Resilience

Each time we embrace change, we build our resilience. Resilience is the ability to adapt and bounce back from life's challenges, and it's a skill that grows stronger the more we practice it. When we face change head-on and learn to navigate it with grace, we become more confident in our ability to handle future challenges.

Resilience doesn't mean that change is easy or painless—it means that we have the inner strength to weather the storms of life and emerge stronger on the other side. By learning to embrace change, we develop the mental and emotional resilience needed to thrive in a constantly evolving world.

Quote from Viktor Frankl:
"When we are no longer able to change a situation, we are challenged to change ourselves."
This quote reminds us that while we can't always control external circumstances, we can control how we respond to them, and that change often presents an opportunity for inner growth.

Section 3: Practical Strategies for Embracing Change

Embracing change doesn't mean pretending that it's easy or avoiding the discomfort that comes with it. It means learning to navigate change with mindfulness, flexibility, and an open heart. In this section, we'll explore practical strategies for letting go of resistance and embracing change in your life.

3.1 Cultivating a Growth Mindset

A growth mindset, as defined by psychologist **Carol Dweck**, is the belief that our abilities and intelligence can be developed through effort, learning, and perseverance. This mindset is essential for embracing change, as it encourages us to view challenges as opportunities for growth, rather than threats to our security.

When we approach change with a growth mindset, we see setbacks and difficulties as part of the learning process. Instead of fearing failure, we embrace the idea that mistakes are opportunities to improve and adapt.

Exercise: Shifting to a Growth Mindset in the Face of Change
- **Instructions**: Think about a change you're currently experiencing or anticipating. Write down any fears or concerns you have about this change—whether it's fear of failure, loss, or discomfort. Now,

reframe each fear through the lens of a growth mindset. For example, if you're afraid of failing at a new job, reframe it as, "This job will help me develop new skills, and any challenges I face will be opportunities to grow." By shifting your perspective, you can approach change with more confidence and openness.
- **Reflection**: How did reframing your fears through a growth mindset help you feel more empowered in the face of change? How can adopting this mindset help you embrace future challenges with a sense of curiosity and resilience?

3.2 Letting Go of Control

As discussed earlier, one of the main reasons we resist change is the fear of losing control. However, control is often an illusion. We can't control everything that happens in life, but we can control how we respond to it. Letting go of the need to control every outcome allows us to flow with change, rather than resist it. This doesn't mean giving up or becoming passive—it means accepting that uncertainty is a natural part of life and trusting in our ability to adapt to whatever comes our way.

Exercise: The Letting Go Meditation
- **Instructions**: Set aside 10-15 minutes for a letting go meditation. Sit in a comfortable position, close your eyes, and take a few deep breaths. As you breathe in, visualize yourself drawing in a sense of calm and acceptance. As you breathe out, imagine letting go of any need for control, releasing your fears, anxieties, or resistance to change. With each exhale, mentally repeat the words "I let go." Allow yourself to simply be present with the sensation of releasing control. If specific worries or fears come to mind, acknowledge them, and then visualize them drifting away with your breath.
- **Reflection**: After completing the meditation, reflect on how it felt to consciously let go of control. Did it help you feel lighter or more at peace with the uncertainty in your life? How can this practice of letting go help you approach change with greater trust in your ability to adapt?

3.3 Practicing Acceptance

Acceptance is a key component of embracing change. When we practice acceptance, we stop resisting the reality of the situation and instead choose to work with it. This doesn't mean that we have to like or agree with the changes happening in our lives, but it does mean that we acknowledge them as part of our current reality.

By accepting change, we stop wasting energy on fighting what is beyond our control. Instead, we can focus on finding solutions, adapting, and moving forward.

Exercise: Radical Acceptance Journal
- **Instructions**: Choose an area of your life where you are struggling to accept change—whether it's a career transition, a relationship shift, or a personal challenge. Write down any feelings of resistance you have toward this change. Next, write a statement of acceptance, such as, "I accept that this change is happening, even though it's difficult." Reflect on how you can begin to work with this change, rather than resist it. Consider what steps you can take to adapt or what positive outcomes might come from embracing the change.
- **Reflection**: How did writing a statement of acceptance affect your perspective on the change? Did it help you feel more at peace or open to new possibilities? How can practicing acceptance regularly help you navigate future changes with less resistance?

3.4 Seeking Support

While embracing change is a personal journey, it's important to remember that you don't have to go through it alone. Seeking support from friends, family, or a therapist can provide valuable perspective and emotional support during times of transition. Talking through your feelings with others can help you process the change and gain clarity on how to move forward.

Additionally, surrounding yourself with people who have successfully navigated change can inspire and motivate you to embrace your own transitions with courage and optimism.

Exercise: Reaching Out for Support
- **Instructions**: Think of someone in your life who has been through a significant change and come out stronger. Reach out to this person and ask if they'd be willing to share their experience with you. What strategies did they use to navigate change? How did they cope with uncertainty or fear? If you're feeling overwhelmed by a particular change in your life, consider talking to a trusted friend or therapist for guidance and support.
- **Reflection**: How did seeking support impact your outlook on the change you're experiencing? Did hearing about someone else's journey help you feel more hopeful or empowered? How can you

continue to lean on your support network during times of change?

Section 4: The Role of Mindfulness in Embracing Change

Mindfulness is a powerful practice for staying grounded in the present moment, especially during times of change. When we face uncertainty or transition, our minds often race ahead to future worries or dwell on past regrets. Mindfulness helps us return to the present, where we can find peace, clarity, and the ability to respond to change with more calm and intention.

4.1 Staying Present in the Midst of Change

Change often triggers anxiety because it pulls us out of the present moment. We become consumed by thoughts of what might happen or what we fear losing. Mindfulness helps us refocus our attention on the here and now, allowing us to experience the present without being overwhelmed by fears of the future.

Exercise: Mindful Breathing for Grounding During Change
- **Instructions**: Whenever you find yourself feeling anxious or overwhelmed by change, take a few moments to practice mindful breathing. Sit comfortably, close your eyes, and focus on your breath. As you inhale, count to four. Hold your breath for a count of four, then exhale for a count of four. Repeat this cycle for five to ten minutes, keeping your attention on the rhythm of your breath. If your mind begins to wander, gently bring your focus back to your breath.
- **Reflection**: How did practicing mindful breathing help you feel more grounded in the present moment? Did it reduce feelings of anxiety or overwhelm? How can you use this mindfulness practice to stay present and calm during times of change?

4.2 Observing Without Judgment

One of the key principles of mindfulness is non-judgmental awareness—observing your thoughts and emotions without labeling them as good or bad. When you face change, you may experience a wide range of emotions, from fear and frustration to excitement and hope. Practicing non-judgmental awareness allows you to experience these emotions fully without getting caught up in self-criticism or judgment.

Exercise: Mindful Observation of Emotions
- **Instructions**: The next time you feel overwhelmed by change, take a moment to observe your emotions without judgment. Sit quietly and

notice what you're feeling—whether it's anxiety, sadness, anger, or joy. Instead of labeling these emotions as "good" or "bad," simply acknowledge them as part of your experience. Say to yourself, "I'm feeling [emotion] right now, and that's okay." Allow the emotions to be present without trying to change or fix them.
- **Reflection**: How did observing your emotions without judgment affect your experience of the change? Did it help you feel more at ease or more accepting of your emotions? How can this practice of non-judgmental awareness help you navigate future changes with greater emotional balance?

Section 5: Embracing Life's Transitions

Life is filled with transitions—some are planned, while others are unexpected. From moving to a new city or starting a new job to navigating the loss of a loved one or ending a relationship, transitions mark significant changes in our lives. Learning to embrace these transitions with openness and resilience can help us navigate life's ups and downs with greater ease.

5.1 Viewing Transitions as Transformative

Transitions are often seen as periods of uncertainty or loss, but they can also be times of profound transformation. When we go through a significant life transition, we are given the opportunity to reexamine our values, redefine our goals, and grow in ways we never imagined. While transitions may be uncomfortable or even painful, they can also serve as catalysts for positive change.

Exercise: Reframing a Life Transition
- **Instructions**: Think of a major transition you are currently experiencing or have recently experienced. Write down any challenges or difficulties you've faced as a result of this transition. Next, reframe the transition by identifying any opportunities for growth or positive change that may arise from it. For example, if you're moving to a new city, consider how this transition might open the door to new relationships, experiences, or career opportunities.
- **Reflection**: How did reframing the transition help you feel more hopeful or optimistic about the changes in your life? What lessons or opportunities might emerge from this transition, and how can you embrace them with openness and curiosity?

5.2 Rituals for Marking Transitions

Throughout history, people have used rituals to mark significant transitions in their lives—whether it's a graduation, a wedding, or a funeral. These rituals help us process the changes we're experiencing and provide a sense of closure or celebration. Creating your own personal rituals for transitions can help you navigate change with intention and meaning.

Exercise: Creating a Transition Ritual
- **Instructions**: Choose a transition you are currently going through—whether it's starting a new job, moving to a new home, or ending a relationship. Create a personal ritual to mark this transition. This could be as simple as lighting a candle and reflecting on your journey, writing a letter to yourself about the lessons you've learned, or creating a vision board for your next chapter. The ritual should feel meaningful and personal to you.
- **Reflection**: How did performing a transition ritual help you process the change? Did it provide a sense of closure or intention for moving forward? How can incorporating rituals into your life help you embrace future transitions with more clarity and purpose?

Conclusion to Chapter 6: The Freedom in Embracing Change

Change is a natural part of life, and learning to embrace it is essential for personal growth, happiness, and fulfillment. While change often brings uncertainty, discomfort, and even fear, it also brings opportunities for transformation, new experiences, and resilience.

By cultivating a growth mindset, practicing mindfulness, and letting go of the need for control, you can learn to navigate life's changes with grace and openness. Embracing change doesn't mean that it will always be easy, but it does mean trusting in your ability to adapt and thrive in the face of uncertainty.

As you move forward, remember that every change—whether welcomed or unplanned—is an opportunity for growth and renewal. By embracing life's transitions, you create space for new possibilities and allow yourself to fully experience the richness of life's journey.

In the next chapter, we'll explore how building resilience through self-care can help you stay strong, balanced, and centered during times of change and uncertainty. By prioritizing your well-being, you'll create a solid foundation for facing life's challenges with confidence and strength.

Chapter 7: Building Resilience Through Self-Care

Introduction to Resilience and Self-Care

Resilience is the ability to bounce back from adversity, to navigate life's challenges with strength, and to emerge from difficult situations with a sense of growth. In a world where change is constant and uncertainty is inevitable, resilience is a vital skill that allows us to face adversity with confidence and grace.

But resilience doesn't happen in isolation—it is something we cultivate over time, and it is deeply linked to self-care. At its core, resilience is about how we take care of ourselves, mentally, emotionally, physically, and spiritually, during difficult times. When we prioritize self-care, we build the internal resources needed to cope with stress, manage change, and thrive in the face of adversity.

This chapter will explore how self-care is the foundation for resilience, offering practical strategies for nurturing your body, mind, and spirit. By committing to your well-being, you create the resilience needed to navigate life's ups and downs with balance, strength, and peace.

Section 1: Understanding Resilience

Before diving into self-care practices, it's important to understand what resilience truly means and why it's essential for navigating life's challenges. Resilience is not about being tough or never feeling vulnerable. Instead, it's about flexibility, adaptability, and the ability to recover from setbacks.

1.1 The Core Components of Resilience

Resilience can be broken down into several key components that work together to help us manage stress, recover from challenges, and grow through adversity:
1. **Emotional Regulation**: The ability to manage and process emotions in a healthy way, rather than becoming overwhelmed by stress, anxiety, or anger.
2. **Mental Flexibility**: The ability to adapt to changing circumstances, stay open to new ideas, and approach problems with creativity and resourcefulness.
3. **Self-Efficacy**: A sense of confidence in one's ability to handle life's

challenges, grounded in the belief that you have the skills and resources needed to cope with adversity.
4. **Support Systems**: Relationships with family, friends, and community that provide emotional, practical, and social support during difficult times.
5. **Purpose and Meaning**: Having a sense of purpose or meaning in life that provides motivation, direction, and a reason to persevere through hardships.

Quote from Viktor Frankl:
"When we are no longer able to change a situation, we are challenged to change ourselves."
This quote encapsulates the essence of resilience—learning to grow and adapt when faced with situations beyond our control.

1.2 The Role of Self-Care in Resilience

Self-care is the foundation upon which resilience is built. Without regular self-care, our ability to cope with stress and adversity is diminished. Self-care provides the mental, emotional, and physical resources we need to recover from setbacks, manage challenges, and sustain our well-being over time.

Self-care is often misunderstood as indulgence or luxury, but it is, in fact, a necessity. It involves making time for rest, nourishing your body, nurturing your mind, and creating space for activities that bring you joy and fulfillment. When you prioritize self-care, you build the resilience needed to face life's inevitable challenges with strength and grace.

Exercise: Reflecting on Your Relationship with Resilience and Self-Care
- **Instructions**: Take a few moments to reflect on how you currently respond to challenges or setbacks. Do you feel emotionally and mentally equipped to handle adversity, or do you find yourself easily overwhelmed? Next, consider your self-care habits—how often do you take time to nurture your well-being? Write down how prioritizing self-care might improve your resilience and help you manage challenges with greater ease.
- **Reflection**: How does your current approach to self-care support or hinder your resilience? Are there areas where you could improve your self-care routine to build a stronger foundation for handling adversity?

Section 2: Physical Self-Care for Resilience

Taking care of your physical health is one of the most important aspects of building resilience. When your body is strong, rested, and well-nourished, you have more energy and stamina to handle stress, recover from challenges, and stay grounded during difficult times.

2.1 The Importance of Sleep

Sleep is essential for physical, mental, and emotional resilience. When we are well-rested, our bodies are better equipped to manage stress, our minds are clearer, and our emotional regulation improves. On the other hand, chronic sleep deprivation weakens our ability to cope with stress and increases our vulnerability to anxiety and depression.

Exercise: Creating a Sleep Ritual
- **Instructions**: To improve the quality of your sleep, create a bedtime ritual that helps you unwind and relax. This might include turning off electronic devices an hour before bed, dimming the lights, drinking a cup of herbal tea, or practicing deep breathing or meditation. Stick to a consistent sleep schedule, going to bed and waking up at the same time each day. Track your sleep for a week, noting how you feel physically and mentally after a night of quality rest.
- **Reflection**: How did creating a sleep ritual impact your energy levels, mood, and ability to handle stress? Did it help you feel more rested and resilient throughout the day?

2.2 Nourishing Your Body with Healthy Foods

The food we eat directly affects our physical and mental resilience. A balanced, nutrient-rich diet supports your immune system, helps regulate your mood, and provides the energy needed to face challenges. On the other hand, poor nutrition can lead to fatigue, irritability, and weakened mental and emotional resilience.

Exercise: Mindful Eating for Resilience
- **Instructions**: For the next week, practice mindful eating by paying attention to the foods you consume and how they affect your energy levels and mood. Focus on incorporating whole, nutrient-dense foods such as fruits, vegetables, whole grains, and lean proteins into your meals. As you eat, take the time to savor the flavors and textures, and notice how different foods make you feel. Avoid processed foods that may cause energy crashes or irritability.

- **Reflection**: How did practicing mindful eating affect your physical and emotional well-being? Did eating more nutritious foods help you feel more energized, focused, or resilient? How can continuing this practice support your overall health and ability to handle stress?

2.3 The Power of Physical Activity

Exercise is a powerful tool for building resilience, as it reduces stress, improves mood, and boosts overall well-being. Regular physical activity helps regulate stress hormones such as cortisol and adrenaline while increasing the production of endorphins—chemicals in the brain that promote feelings of happiness and relaxation.

Exercise: Finding Joy in Movement
- **Instructions**: Choose a form of physical activity that you enjoy—whether it's yoga, walking, dancing, swimming, or strength training—and commit to doing it regularly. Aim for at least 30 minutes of movement each day, and notice how it impacts your energy, mood, and resilience. Focus on the joy of movement rather than perfection or performance. If you can, spend time exercising in nature, as being outdoors can enhance the stress-reducing benefits of physical activity.
- **Reflection**: How did incorporating regular physical activity into your routine impact your stress levels and overall resilience? Did moving your body help you feel more grounded, energized, or able to handle challenges with greater ease?

Section 3: Mental and Emotional Self-Care for Resilience

In addition to caring for your physical health, mental and emotional self-care is essential for building resilience. When we take time to nurture our minds and emotions, we strengthen our ability to manage stress, process difficult feelings, and stay mentally flexible in the face of adversity.

3.1 Practicing Mindfulness for Emotional Resilience

Mindfulness is the practice of bringing your attention to the present moment without judgment. By cultivating mindfulness, you develop the ability to observe your thoughts and emotions without being overwhelmed by them. This helps you respond to stress and challenges with greater clarity and calm.

Exercise: The 5-Minute Mindfulness Practice

- **Instructions**: Set aside 5 minutes each day for a mindfulness practice. Find a quiet space where you won't be interrupted, sit comfortably, and close your eyes. Focus on your breath, noticing the sensation of the air as it enters and leaves your body. If your mind begins to wander, gently bring your focus back to your breath without judgment. As you practice mindfulness, observe any thoughts or emotions that arise without trying to change or control them—simply let them pass.
- **Reflection**: How did practicing mindfulness help you feel more centered or calm? Did it reduce feelings of stress or anxiety? How can continuing this practice support your emotional resilience in the face of challenges?

3.2 Journaling for Mental Clarity

Journaling is a powerful tool for processing emotions, gaining mental clarity, and building resilience. Writing about your thoughts and feelings helps externalize your worries, allowing you to reflect on them from a new perspective. It can also help you identify patterns in your thinking, set goals, and track your progress in handling stress.

Exercise: The Daily Journaling Practice
- **Instructions**: Set aside 10-15 minutes each day to journal. Write about any challenges or stresses you're currently facing, as well as your thoughts and emotions surrounding them. Don't worry about grammar or structure—just let the words flow. You can also use journaling prompts such as "What am I grateful for today?" or "What steps can I take to manage this challenge?" After journaling, take a few moments to reflect on how you feel.
- **Reflection**: How did journaling help you process your emotions or gain clarity about the challenges you're facing? Did it provide relief, insight, or a sense of empowerment? How can you use this practice to track your personal growth, navigate difficult emotions, and build resilience over time?

3.3 Cultivating Self-Compassion

Self-compassion is essential for emotional resilience. Many of us are our own harshest critics, especially during times of stress or failure. When we practice self-compassion, we treat ourselves with the same kindness and understanding that we would offer to a friend in need. Self-compassion helps us recover from setbacks more quickly and with greater emotional balance.

According to **Dr. Kristin Neff**, a leading researcher on self-compassion, the practice consists of three main elements:
1. **Self-kindness**: Being gentle and understanding with yourself rather than harshly self-critical.
2. **Common humanity**: Recognizing that suffering and imperfection are a shared part of the human experience, and you are not alone in your struggles.
3. **Mindfulness**: Observing your thoughts and feelings without becoming overwhelmed by them or judging yourself for having them.

Exercise: Practicing Self-Compassion
- **Instructions**: The next time you experience a setback, failure, or challenge, pause and acknowledge your suffering. Instead of criticizing yourself, offer yourself kindness. You might say, "This is really hard right now, but I'm doing the best I can," or "It's okay to feel upset—I'm not alone in this struggle." Place your hand over your heart and take a few deep breaths, allowing yourself to feel supported by your own kindness and compassion.
- **Reflection**: How did practicing self-compassion change the way you responded to a challenge or setback? Did it help you feel more emotionally balanced or supported? How can you continue to cultivate self-compassion in moments of stress or difficulty?

3.4 Building Mental Flexibility

Resilience is closely tied to mental flexibility—the ability to adapt your thinking and behavior in response to new information or changing circumstances. Mental flexibility helps you approach problems with creativity and openness rather than getting stuck in rigid thinking or habits. When you develop this skill, you become more resilient in the face of uncertainty and change.

Exercise: Reframing Negative Thoughts
- **Instructions**: The next time you find yourself stuck in a negative thought pattern, such as "I'll never be able to handle this" or "This situation is hopeless," practice reframing the thought. Ask yourself, "What is another way of looking at this situation?" or "What opportunities might arise from this challenge?" Write down a more balanced or hopeful perspective, and reflect on how this new perspective might help you approach the situation with greater mental flexibility.

- **Reflection**: How did reframing your thoughts change the way you felt about the challenge? Did it open up new possibilities or solutions? How can practicing mental flexibility help you stay resilient in the face of life's uncertainties?

Section 4: Spiritual and Social Self-Care for Resilience

Resilience is not only about managing stress on your own—it's also about connecting to sources of meaning, purpose, and support. Nurturing your spiritual well-being and cultivating strong social connections provide an essential foundation for resilience during difficult times.

4.1 Finding Meaning and Purpose

A sense of meaning and purpose is a powerful source of resilience. When you have a deeper sense of why you're doing what you're doing, it becomes easier to persevere through difficult times. Purpose gives you the motivation to keep going, even when the path is challenging.

For some, this sense of purpose comes from their work, relationships, or personal goals. For others, it may be connected to their spiritual or religious beliefs. Whatever your source of purpose, nurturing it can help you stay grounded and resilient in the face of adversity.

Exercise: Reflecting on Your Purpose
- **Instructions**: Take some time to reflect on what gives your life meaning and purpose. Write down three things that bring you a sense of fulfillment or direction—whether it's your work, family, creative projects, or spiritual beliefs. Reflect on how these sources of purpose have helped you navigate past challenges, and consider how they can continue to support your resilience in the future.
- **Reflection**: How does connecting to your sense of purpose help you stay resilient during difficult times? How can nurturing these sources of meaning provide motivation and strength in the face of future challenges?

4.2 Strengthening Social Connections

Strong social connections are one of the most important factors in building resilience. When we are supported by friends, family, and community, we feel more grounded and less isolated during times of stress. Relationships provide emotional support, practical help, and a sense of belonging, all of which are crucial for managing adversity.

However, building and maintaining relationships requires effort, especially during busy or stressful times. It's important to invest in your relationships, both by reaching out for support when you need it and by offering support to others.

Exercise: Strengthening Your Support Network
- **Instructions**: Take stock of your current support network. Write down the names of the people you can rely on for emotional support, practical help, or companionship. Next, reach out to one or two people in your support network—whether through a phone call, text, or in-person visit. Let them know you appreciate their presence in your life, and offer your support in return. Consider making it a regular practice to nurture these relationships.
- **Reflection**: How did reaching out to your support network affect your sense of connection and resilience? Did it remind you that you're not alone in facing challenges? How can continuing to strengthen your relationships help you stay grounded and supported during difficult times?

4.3 Nurturing Your Spiritual Well-Being

For many people, spirituality is an important source of strength and resilience. Whether through meditation, prayer, time in nature, or involvement in a religious community, spiritual practices can provide comfort, guidance, and a sense of connection to something greater than oneself.

Spiritual well-being doesn't have to be tied to organized religion—it can be about whatever helps you feel connected, grounded, and at peace. Engaging in regular spiritual practices can help you find meaning in adversity, cultivate inner peace, and foster resilience during challenging times.

Exercise: Creating a Spiritual Practice
- **Instructions**: If you don't already have a regular spiritual practice, take some time to reflect on what activities help you feel spiritually connected. This could include meditation, prayer, journaling, spending time in nature, or participating in a religious or spiritual community. Choose one practice to engage in regularly, whether it's daily, weekly, or whenever you feel the need for grounding. Notice how this practice helps you stay resilient during times of stress or uncertainty.

- **Reflection**: How did engaging in a spiritual practice affect your sense of peace and resilience? Did it help you feel more grounded or connected to something larger than yourself? How can continuing this practice support your overall well-being and ability to handle life's challenges?

Conclusion to Chapter 7: Cultivating Resilience Through Self-Care

Resilience is not a trait that some people are born with and others are not—it is something that we can all cultivate through intentional self-care. By taking care of your body, mind, emotions, and spirit, you build the internal resources needed to navigate life's challenges with strength, grace, and balance.

Self-care is not selfish—it is the foundation of resilience. When you prioritize your well-being, you are better equipped to handle stress, recover from setbacks, and stay grounded during times of uncertainty. Through practices such as mindful eating, exercise, sleep, journaling, mindfulness, self-compassion, and spiritual connection, you nurture the resilience needed to thrive in an ever-changing world.

As you move forward, remember that resilience is a journey, not a destination. By regularly investing in your self-care, you will continue to grow stronger and more adaptable, ready to face life's challenges with an open heart and a resilient spirit.

In the next chapter, we will explore the importance of cultivating gratitude and how practicing gratitude can shift your mindset, improve your well-being, and help you build a more resilient and joyful life. By focusing on what you have, rather than what you lack, you will discover the power of gratitude to transform both your inner and outer world.

Chapter 8: Cultivating Gratitude for a Resilient and Joyful Life

Introduction to Gratitude

Gratitude is one of the most powerful practices for fostering resilience, improving mental health, and creating a more joyful life. At its core, gratitude is the practice of appreciating the good in our lives—whether it's the people we love, the opportunities we've been given, or the simple pleasures of each day. When we cultivate gratitude, we shift our focus from what we lack to what we have, which helps us build emotional resilience and stay grounded during difficult times.

In this chapter, we'll explore how cultivating gratitude can transform your mindset, deepen your sense of well-being, and help you build resilience in the face of adversity. We'll also look at practical ways to incorporate gratitude into your daily life, both through formal practices like journaling and through informal moments of mindful appreciation.

Section 1: The Science of Gratitude

Gratitude is more than just a feel-good emotion—it's a practice backed by scientific research. Numerous studies have shown that gratitude has a wide range of benefits for both mental and physical health. Understanding the science behind gratitude can help motivate you to incorporate this powerful practice into your daily life.

1.1 The Psychological Benefits of Gratitude

Research in positive psychology has found that gratitude is strongly associated with increased happiness, reduced depression, and greater life satisfaction. People who regularly practice gratitude tend to experience more positive emotions, feel more connected to others, and are more resilient in the face of stress and adversity.

Dr. Robert Emmons, one of the world's leading researchers on gratitude, has conducted numerous studies showing that gratitude boosts psychological well-being. His research has found that people who keep gratitude journals report higher levels of optimism, joy, and contentment, as well as lower levels of envy, anxiety, and resentment.

1.2 The Physical Health Benefits of Gratitude

Gratitude doesn't just improve mental health—it also has a positive impact on physical well-being. Studies have shown that people who practice gratitude regularly experience fewer physical symptoms, such as headaches, fatigue, and gastrointestinal problems. Gratitude has also been linked to better sleep quality, lower blood pressure, and improved immune function.

One study published in the **Journal of Psychosomatic Research** found that people who practiced gratitude for just two weeks reported fewer physical complaints and better overall health. Another study from the **University of California, Davis** showed that people who kept a daily gratitude journal slept better, exercised more, and had fewer doctor visits compared to those who didn't.

Quote from Dr. Robert Emmons:
"Gratitude is an affirmation of goodness. We affirm that there are good things in the world, gifts and benefits we've received, and we recognize that the sources of this goodness are outside of ourselves." This quote highlights the essence of gratitude—it's not just about recognizing good things but also about acknowledging the interconnectedness of life and the people, experiences, and circumstances that contribute to our well-being.

Section 2: How Gratitude Builds Resilience

Gratitude and resilience are closely linked. When we cultivate gratitude, we strengthen our ability to cope with challenges, recover from setbacks, and stay grounded during difficult times. Gratitude shifts our focus from what's going wrong to what's going right, helping us maintain perspective and find hope, even in the face of adversity.

2.1 Gratitude as a Tool for Reframing Challenges

One of the most powerful ways gratitude builds resilience is by helping us reframe challenges. When we practice gratitude, we train our minds to look for the good in every situation, even when things are tough. This doesn't mean ignoring or minimizing difficulties—it means recognizing that even in hard times, there are still things to be grateful for, whether it's the support of loved ones, the lessons we're learning, or the strength we're developing.

Example:

Imagine you've lost your job, and you're feeling overwhelmed by uncertainty and fear. While it's natural to focus on the negative aspects of the situation, gratitude can help you shift your perspective. Instead of dwelling solely on the loss, you might choose to be grateful for the new opportunities this change could bring—perhaps it's a chance to explore a different career path, develop new skills, or spend more time with family. Gratitude helps you see challenges as opportunities for growth and transformation.

2.2 Gratitude and Emotional Regulation

Gratitude also plays a key role in emotional regulation, which is a crucial aspect of resilience. When we practice gratitude, we activate the brain's reward centers, releasing feel-good neurotransmitters like dopamine and serotonin. This helps regulate negative emotions like anxiety, frustration, and anger, making it easier to stay calm and balanced during stressful situations.

Gratitude encourages us to focus on the present moment, which reduces rumination and negative thinking. By bringing our attention to the positive aspects of our lives, we shift our mindset from one of scarcity to one of abundance, which fosters greater emotional resilience and well-being.

2.3 Gratitude Strengthens Social Connections

Resilience is not just about individual strength—it's also about the support we receive from others. Gratitude strengthens our social connections by helping us appreciate the people in our lives and express our thanks for their support. When we practice gratitude, we foster deeper relationships, which provide a crucial source of emotional and practical support during tough times.

Case Study:

Consider the story of Sarah, who was going through a difficult divorce. At first, she felt isolated and overwhelmed, but as she began to practice gratitude, she started to notice the support she was receiving from friends and family.

She began expressing her appreciation to those who were helping her, and in return, her relationships deepened. This network of support became a crucial part of Sarah's ability to navigate the emotional challenges of her divorce with resilience.

Section 3: Practical Gratitude Practices for Building Resilience

Cultivating gratitude is not just a mental exercise—it's something you can actively practice in your daily life. In this section, we'll explore a variety of practical gratitude practices that can help you build resilience and enhance your well-being.

3.1 Gratitude Journaling

One of the most well-researched and effective gratitude practices is keeping a gratitude journal. This simple yet powerful practice involves writing down a few things you're grateful for each day. By reflecting on the positive aspects of your life, you train your brain to focus on what's going right, even during challenging times.

Exercise: The Daily Gratitude Journal
- **Instructions**: Set aside a few minutes each day to write in your gratitude journal. Each day, list three to five things you're grateful for. These can be big or small—from a kind gesture from a friend to the beauty of a sunset. The key is to focus on specific things that brought you joy, comfort, or peace that day. Try to vary your entries each day to keep your mind actively engaged in seeking out new things to appreciate.
- **Reflection**: After a week of gratitude journaling, reflect on how this practice has impacted your mindset. Did it help you focus more on the positive aspects of your life? Did it help you feel more resilient or hopeful in the face of challenges?

3.2 Gratitude Letters

Another powerful gratitude practice is writing a letter to someone you're grateful for, expressing your appreciation for their presence in your life. This practice not only strengthens your relationships but also increases your own feelings of happiness and connection.

Exercise: Writing a Gratitude Letter
- **Instructions**: Think of someone in your life—whether a friend, family member, teacher, or mentor—who has had a positive impact on you. Write a letter expressing your gratitude for their kindness, support, or guidance. Be specific about what you appreciate and how they've made a difference in your life. If you feel comfortable, consider delivering the letter in person or reading it aloud to them. If that's not possible, you can send it via mail or email.

- **Reflection**: How did writing a gratitude letter affect your feelings of connection and appreciation? Did expressing your gratitude to someone else deepen your relationship or help you feel more supported? How can this practice strengthen your resilience through the power of social connection?

3.3 Mindful Moments of Gratitude

Gratitude doesn't always have to be formal—it can be as simple as taking a few mindful moments throughout the day to appreciate the good things around you. By cultivating the habit of pausing to notice small blessings, you create a more grateful mindset that can help you stay resilient in the face of stress.

Exercise: Practicing Mindful Gratitude
- **Instructions**: Throughout the day, practice pausing to notice small moments of beauty, joy, or comfort. For example, you might take a moment to appreciate the warmth of your morning coffee, the sound of birds outside your window, or the smile of a colleague. Each time you notice something you're grateful for, take a deep breath and silently express your thanks.
- **Reflection**: How did practicing mindful gratitude affect your awareness of the present moment? Did it help you feel more grounded, calm, or appreciative throughout the day? How can this practice support your emotional resilience, especially during stressful times?

3.4 Gratitude Rituals for Difficult Times

It can be challenging to practice gratitude during difficult times, but it's precisely during these moments that gratitude can be most transformative. Developing gratitude rituals that help you focus on the good, even when life feels overwhelming, can help you maintain a sense of balance and perspective.

Exercise: Creating a Gratitude Ritual
- **Instructions**: During a challenging time, create a gratitude ritual to help ground yourself. This could involve lighting a candle and reflecting on three things you're grateful for, taking a walk in nature while focusing on the beauty around you, or saying a simple gratitude prayer or affirmation each morning. Choose a ritual that resonates with you and commit to practicing it regularly, especially when you're feeling stressed or overwhelmed.

- **Reflection**: How did incorporating a gratitude ritual into your routine help you navigate difficult emotions or situations? Did it provide comfort, perspective, or a sense of peace? How can this practice become a part of your self-care toolkit for building resilience in the face of future challenges?

Section 4: Cultivating Gratitude in Relationships

Gratitude isn't just about individual well-being—it also plays a critical role in building and maintaining strong, healthy relationships. When we express gratitude toward others, we reinforce feelings of connection, trust, and mutual appreciation. Cultivating gratitude in relationships helps strengthen the emotional bonds that support us through life's ups and downs.

4.1 Expressing Gratitude to Loved Ones

In the busyness of daily life, it's easy to take the people we love for granted. However, expressing gratitude to those who support us—whether it's family, friends, or partners—can deepen our relationships and foster a greater sense of connection. When we acknowledge the positive impact others have on our lives, we create an atmosphere of appreciation that strengthens emotional intimacy and trust.

Exercise: The Gratitude Conversation
- **Instructions**: Choose a loved one you'd like to express gratitude to—whether it's a partner, parent, sibling, or close friend. Set aside time for a conversation where you focus on expressing your appreciation for them. Be specific about what you value in your relationship and how they've supported or enriched your life. Pay attention to their response, and allow this conversation to deepen your bond.
- **Reflection**: How did expressing gratitude to a loved one affect your relationship? Did it create a stronger sense of connection or appreciation? How can regularly expressing gratitude to the people in your life help you build more resilient, supportive relationships?

4.2 Creating a Culture of Gratitude in Your Relationships

Gratitude can also play a role in creating a positive, supportive atmosphere in your relationships. When both partners or family members practice gratitude, it can reduce conflict, increase emotional support, and promote a deeper sense of trust and connection. Creating a culture of gratitude in your relationships means regularly expressing appreciation and focusing on each other's strengths rather than weaknesses.

Exercise: Gratitude Check-Ins with a Partner or Family Member
- **Instructions**: If you're in a relationship or living with family members, consider incorporating regular gratitude check-ins into your routine. This could be a weekly practice where you take a few moments to share what you appreciate about each other, express thanks for any acts of kindness or support, or acknowledge positive changes or growth in your relationship. This practice helps reinforce positive behaviors and deepens your emotional connection.
- **Reflection**: How did practicing regular gratitude check-ins affect your relationship dynamics? Did it create a more supportive, positive environment? How can continuing this practice help you build a stronger, more resilient relationship?

4.3 Gratitude as a Tool for Conflict Resolution

Gratitude can also be a powerful tool for resolving conflict in relationships. When we focus on what we appreciate about the other person, it becomes easier to navigate disagreements with empathy and understanding. Gratitude shifts the focus from criticism to appreciation, making it easier to find common ground and work toward solutions.

Exercise: Using Gratitude to Navigate Conflict
- **Instructions**: The next time you experience conflict with a loved one, take a moment to reflect on what you appreciate about the person. Before addressing the issue, express gratitude for something they've done recently or for a positive quality they bring to the relationship. Then, approach the conflict with an attitude of collaboration, rather than blame. Focus on finding a solution that benefits both parties while maintaining mutual respect.
- **Reflection**: How did expressing gratitude during a conflict change the tone of the conversation? Did it help reduce tension or foster a more cooperative approach? How can incorporating gratitude into your conflict resolution strategies improve communication and strengthen your relationships?

Section 5: Gratitude in Challenging Times
Gratitude is often most transformative when practiced during difficult times. It can be hard to feel grateful when you're facing loss, disappointment, or

hardship, but it's precisely during these moments that gratitude can provide a sense of perspective, hope, and emotional resilience. By focusing on what remains good or meaningful, even in the midst of adversity, gratitude helps you maintain balance and optimism.

5.1 Gratitude as a Coping Mechanism for Stress and Anxiety

When we're overwhelmed by stress or anxiety, it's easy to get caught up in negative thinking. Gratitude offers a way to counterbalance these negative emotions by shifting your focus to the positive aspects of your life. This practice doesn't eliminate stress or anxiety, but it helps you manage it more effectively by reminding you of the resources, strengths, and support systems you have.

Exercise: Gratitude Breathing for Stress Relief
- **Instructions**: The next time you're feeling stressed or anxious, take a few moments to practice gratitude breathing. Sit quietly and close your eyes. As you inhale, think of something you're grateful for—whether it's a supportive friend, a recent accomplishment, or a simple pleasure like the warmth of the sun. As you exhale, release any tension or worry. Repeat this cycle for five to ten minutes, focusing on a different source of gratitude with each breath.
- **Reflection**: How did practicing gratitude breathing affect your stress or anxiety levels? Did it help you feel more grounded or calm? How can using this practice regularly help you manage stress and stay resilient during challenging times?

5.2 Gratitude and Loss: Finding Meaning in Adversity

Gratitude can be particularly difficult to practice in the face of loss, whether it's the loss of a loved one, a job, or a significant life change. However, gratitude doesn't mean ignoring or minimizing grief—it's about finding meaning in adversity. By focusing on the lessons learned, the love shared, or the ways in which the experience has shaped you, gratitude can help you process loss in a way that honors both the pain and the growth that comes from it.

Exercise: Gratitude Reflection for Loss
- **Instructions**: If you're experiencing loss, take some time to reflect on what you're grateful for in relation to the person or situation. This might include the memories you shared, the lessons you learned, or the strength you've gained from the experience. Write these reflections down in a journal or share them with a trusted friend or

therapist. Allow yourself to feel both the grief and the gratitude, knowing that both emotions can coexist.
- **Reflection**: How did reflecting on gratitude in the midst of loss affect your healing process? Did it help you find meaning or comfort, even in the pain? How can continuing to practice gratitude help you honor the experience while moving forward with resilience?

5.3 Gratitude as a Tool for Overcoming Disappointment

Disappointment is a natural part of life, whether it's a missed opportunity, an unmet goal, or a setback in your personal or professional life. While it's important to acknowledge and process feelings of disappointment, gratitude can help you shift your perspective and focus on the opportunities that still exist. By recognizing the things that are still going well, you build emotional resilience and avoid getting stuck in negative thinking.

Exercise: The Gratitude Shift for Disappointment
- **Instructions**: The next time you experience disappointment, take a moment to reflect on what is still going right in your life. Write down three things you're grateful for, even in the midst of the setback. This might include support from loved ones, personal strengths you've developed, or new opportunities on the horizon. By focusing on the positive, you shift your mindset from one of scarcity to one of abundance.
- **Reflection**: How did practicing gratitude in the face of disappointment help you manage your emotions? Did it provide a sense of hope or perspective? How can this practice help you build resilience in the face of future setbacks?

Conclusion to Chapter 8: The Transformative Power of Gratitude
Gratitude is a simple yet powerful practice that has the ability to transform both your inner world and your external circumstances. By focusing on what you have, rather than what you lack, you build resilience, foster stronger relationships, and create a deeper sense of joy and well-being. Gratitude shifts your mindset from one of scarcity to one of abundance, helping you navigate life's challenges with grace, optimism, and hope.

As you continue your journey of personal growth and self-care, remember that gratitude is a practice, not just an emotion. It's something you can actively cultivate each day, whether through journaling, mindful reflection, or expressing appreciation to the people in your life. By making gratitude a regular part of your routine, you will discover its power to uplift your spirit, strengthen your resilience, and bring greater joy to your life.

Conclusion: Living Fully Through Letting Go

As we come to the end of this journey, it's important to reflect on the interconnectedness of the themes we've explored: intentional living, personal growth, mindfulness, resilience, gratitude, and balance. Each concept we've discussed is a crucial thread in the fabric of a life lived with purpose, fulfillment, and joy.

1. The Power of Intentional Living

At the heart of this journey is the idea of intentional living. It is the foundation upon which personal growth, resilience, mindfulness, and balance are built. Living with intention means making conscious choices that align with your core values and long-term vision. It's about breaking free from autopilot and actively creating the life you want, one decision at a time.

By cultivating intention, you step into a life of purpose. You align your actions with what truly matters to you, letting go of societal pressures, distractions, and fear of failure. This intentionality empowers you to navigate life's inevitable challenges with clarity and focus, grounded in a deep understanding of your values and desires.

As you move forward, continue to ask yourself: **What are my core values? How can I make decisions today that reflect these values? What do I want to bring into my life—and what am I ready to let go of?**

2. Lifelong Learning and Personal Growth

Personal growth is an ongoing process, one that requires self-awareness, reflection, and a willingness to evolve. Whether you are learning new skills, exploring your emotional landscape, or embracing new perspectives, personal growth helps you stay curious, adaptable, and open to change. Lifelong learning keeps your mind active and engaged, helping you thrive in a world that is constantly evolving.

Through the practice of personal growth, you unlock your potential and discover new facets of yourself. By cultivating a **growth mindset**, you learn to view challenges as opportunities, setbacks as learning experiences, and life itself as a classroom.

As you reflect on your personal growth journey, ask yourself: **What areas of** my life do I want to grow in? How can I stay open to new learning experiences? How can I approach challenges with curiosity rather than fear?

3. The Role of Mindfulness

Mindfulness, the practice of being fully present in each moment, is the glue that binds intentional living and personal growth together. It allows you to stay connected to the "here and now" and make decisions from a place of clarity, rather than reaction. Mindfulness teaches you to notice your thoughts, emotions, and actions without judgment, giving you the freedom to respond mindfully rather than impulsively.

Incorporating mindfulness into your daily life enhances your sense of calm, improves your focus, and deepens your connection with others. Whether through meditation, mindful breathing, or simply paying attention to your surroundings, mindfulness helps you remain grounded in the present, even during difficult times.

As you continue your mindfulness practice, ask yourself: **How can I bring more presence into my daily life? What moments can I slow down and savor? How can mindfulness help me stay resilient in the face of challenges?**

4. Building Emotional Resilience

Life is full of unexpected challenges, setbacks, and uncertainties. Emotional resilience is the capacity to navigate these ups and downs with strength and grace. Through mindfulness, self-compassion, and gratitude, you can cultivate the resilience needed to bounce back from adversity and continue moving forward.

Resilience is not about avoiding pain or discomfort but about learning to accept and process difficult emotions. It's about trusting that you have the tools and inner strength to overcome obstacles, learn from them, and grow as a result. With emotional resilience, you develop the ability to stay centered in the face of stress, fear, or failure.

As you reflect on your own resilience, ask yourself: **How can I build emotional resilience in my daily life? How can mindfulness and self-compassion help me navigate difficult emotions? What strengths have I developed from past challenges that I can carry forward?**

5. The Power of Gratitude

Gratitude is a transformative practice that shifts your focus from scarcity to abundance. When you cultivate gratitude, you actively recognize the good in your life, whether it's the people around you, the opportunities you've been given, or the simple pleasures of each day. Gratitude helps you stay anchored in the present and fosters a sense of contentment, even in the face of challenges.

Practicing gratitude doesn't mean ignoring difficulties or pretending everything is perfect—it's about acknowledging both the good and the difficult, while choosing to focus on the positive. Gratitude deepens your relationships, enhances your mental and emotional well-being, and brings more joy into your life.

As you explore the practice of gratitude, ask yourself: **What am I grateful for today? How can I express gratitude to those around me? How can I make gratitude a regular part of my daily life?**

6. Achieving Balance in Life

Balance is not about perfection—it's about making adjustments that allow you to honor all areas of your life, from work and relationships to self-care and personal growth. Finding balance means recognizing when one area of your life is taking up too much space and consciously making changes to restore harmony.

Balance allows you to prioritize your well-being without sacrificing your goals or responsibilities. It involves setting boundaries, saying "no" when needed, and ensuring that your time and energy are aligned with your values. When you achieve balance, you create a sense of flow and ease, allowing you to pursue your passions without burning out.

As you strive for balance, ask yourself: **Which areas of my life need more attention? Where do I need to set boundaries? How can I create more harmony between work, relationships, and self-care?**

7. Moving Forward with Intention, Growth, and Mindfulness

The journey toward living an intentional, mindful, and growth-oriented life is an ongoing process. There will be moments of progress, setbacks, and rediscovery along the way. The key is to remain open to the lessons that each moment brings, to approach your journey with curiosity and self-compassion, and to remember that you have the power to shape your life in alignment with your deepest values.

As you move forward, continue to cultivate the practices that support your personal growth, well-being, and fulfillment:

- Live with **intention**, making choices that reflect your values and purpose.
- Embrace **lifelong learning**, staying curious and open to new experiences.
- Practice **mindfulness**, bringing presence and awareness to each moment.
- Cultivate **resilience**, trusting in your ability to navigate life's challenges.
- Nurture **gratitude**, focusing on the abundance in your life.
- Strive for **balance**, honoring all aspects of your well-being.

You are the creator of your own life. Each day is an opportunity to make choices that align with your authentic self, foster growth, and bring you closer to the life you truly desire. As you continue this journey, may you live with intention, embrace growth, practice mindfulness, and find joy in the present moment.

Expanded Workbook: Practical Tools for Intentional Living, Personal Growth, Mindfulness and Letting Go

This expanded workbook is designed to provide you with practical exercises, tools, and reflection prompts to help you integrate the concepts of intentional living, personal growth, mindfulness, and resilience into your everyday life.

Each section corresponds to key themes explored in the chapters, offering you a hands-on approach to applying these principles as you move forward in your journey.

Section 1: Living with Intention

Exercise 1: Defining Your Core Values

Living with intention begins by understanding what matters most to you. This exercise will help you identify your core values and reflect on how to align your life with them.

1. **Instructions**:
    - Take a few moments to reflect on the following questions:
        - What are the qualities or principles that I value most in life?
        - When do I feel most fulfilled or authentic?
        - What drives my decisions and behaviors?
    - From this reflection, write down 5-10 core values that guide your life (e.g., integrity, compassion, creativity, adventure, personal growth).
2. **Reflection**:
    - How do these values show up in your daily life?
    - Are there areas of your life where you are not living in alignment with your values? What changes could you make to bring more alignment?

Exercise 2: Setting Intentional Goals

Now that you've identified your core values, it's time to set goals that align with them.

1. **Instructions**:
    - For each of your core values, set one or two specific, actionable goals that align with those values. Make sure they follow the SMART framework (Specific, Measurable,

Achievable, Relevant, Time-bound).
- Example: If one of your core values is health, a goal might be: "I will exercise for 30 minutes, four times a week for the next three months."
2. **Reflection**:
   - How do these goals support your core values?
   - What steps can you take today to start moving toward these goals?

Section 2: Lifelong Learning and Personal Growth

Exercise 3: Lifelong Learning Plan

Lifelong learning keeps your mind sharp and helps you continue evolving. This exercise will help you create a learning plan that aligns with your personal growth goals.

1. **Instructions**:
   - Identify three areas in which you'd like to grow or learn something new (e.g., career skills, personal hobbies, intellectual pursuits).
   - For each area, write down one action you can take to start learning (e.g., enroll in an online course, read a book, find a mentor).
2. **Reflection**:
   - What excites you most about these learning opportunities?
   - How will learning in these areas contribute to your personal growth?

Exercise 4: Growth Mindset Reflection

Embracing a growth mindset helps you view challenges as opportunities for learning. This exercise will help you reflect on your mindset.

1. **Instructions**:
   - Think of a recent challenge or failure you've experienced.
   - Write down your initial thoughts and reactions to the challenge.
   - Now, reframe the situation: What could you learn from this experience? How can you apply this lesson to future challenges?
2. **Reflection**:
   - How did reframing the challenge through a growth mindset change your perspective?

- How can you continue cultivating a growth mindset in your daily life?

Section 3: Mindfulness and Presence

Exercise 5: Developing a Daily Mindfulness Practice

Mindfulness helps you stay present and grounded. This exercise will guide you in creating a daily mindfulness routine.

1. **Instructions**:
   - Set aside 5-10 minutes each day to practice mindfulness. Choose a time that works best for you (morning, lunch break, or before bed).
   - Start with a simple mindfulness practice like mindful breathing, body scan, or mindful walking.
   - Track your practice in a journal or app, noting how you feel before and after each session.
2. **Reflection**:
   - How did practicing mindfulness affect your stress levels, focus, and emotional state?
   - How can you create consistency in your mindfulness practice?

Exercise 6: Mindful Activity Practice

Mindfulness can be practiced in everyday activities. Choose an activity you do regularly (e.g., eating, walking, brushing your teeth) and practice it mindfully.

1. **Instructions**:
   - Choose one activity (e.g., eating breakfast) and commit to practicing it mindfully for the next week.
   - Pay full attention to the sensations, sights, sounds, and smells involved in the activity. If your mind wanders, gently bring your attention back to the activity.
2. **Reflection**:
   - How did practicing mindfulness in this activity change your experience of it?
   - Did you notice anything new or different about the activity?
   - How can you incorporate mindfulness into more of your daily activities?

Section 4: Emotional Resilience

Exercise 7: Building Emotional Resilience

Resilience is your ability to bounce back from challenges. This exercise will help you strengthen your emotional resilience by reflecting on past experiences.

1. **Instructions**:
   - Think of a time when you faced a significant challenge or setback. Write down how you responded to it emotionally.
   - Now, reflect on what you learned from that experience and how you grew as a result. Write down any strengths or insights you gained.
2. **Reflection**:
   - How has this experience shaped your resilience?
   - What can you do to build resilience in your current life (e.g., self-care, mindfulness, positive self-talk)?

Exercise 8: Emotional Regulation Through Mindfulness

Mindfulness can help you regulate your emotions and prevent being overwhelmed by stress or negative thoughts.

1. **Instructions**:
   - The next time you experience a strong emotion (e.g., anger, frustration, or anxiety), pause and take three deep breaths.
   - Focus on where you feel the emotion in your body (e.g., tightness in your chest, tension in your shoulders). Acknowledge the emotion without judging it.
   - Practice accepting the emotion and allowing it to pass, rather than reacting impulsively.
2. **Reflection**:
   - How did acknowledging and accepting the emotion change your experience of it?
   - How can mindfulness help you manage emotions more effectively in the future?

Section 5: Gratitude Practice

Exercise 9: Daily Gratitude Journal

Gratitude helps you shift your focus from what you lack to what you have. This exercise will help you start a regular gratitude practice.

1. **Instructions**:
   - Each evening, write down three things you are grateful for

    from that day. These can be big or small—anything from a kind gesture to the beauty of nature.
    - Reflect on why you are grateful for each thing and how it positively impacted your day.
2. **Reflection**:
    - How did keeping a gratitude journal affect your mood and mindset?
    - Did it help you focus more on the positive aspects of your life?
    - How can practicing gratitude regularly improve your sense of well-being?

Exercise 10: Expressing Gratitude to Others

Gratitude deepens relationships and fosters connection. This exercise will help you practice expressing gratitude to the people around you.

1. **Instructions**:
    - Think of someone in your life—whether it's a friend, family member, or colleague—who has positively impacted you recently. Write them a letter expressing your gratitude for their support, kindness, or influence.
    - If possible, share the letter with them in person or send it.
2. **Reflection**:
    - How did expressing gratitude to someone else affect your relationship with them?
    - How did it make you feel to reflect on the positive role they've played in your life?
    - How can you continue to cultivate gratitude in your relationships?

Section 6: Finding Balance

Exercise 11: Life Balance Assessment

Balance is about distributing your time and energy in ways that align with your values. This exercise will help you assess the balance in your life.

1. **Instructions**:
    - Draw a circle and divide it into sections that represent different areas of your life (e.g., work, relationships, health, personal growth, leisure). Label each section.
    - Rate your satisfaction with each area of your life on a scale of 1-10, with 1 being very dissatisfied and 10 being very

            satisfied.
        - Reflect on any areas where you feel imbalanced or dissatisfied. What steps can you take to improve balance in these areas?
2. **Reflection**:
    - Which areas of your life are most in need of attention?
    - How can you make adjustments to bring more balance into your daily routine?

Exercise 12: Setting Boundaries for Balance

Setting boundaries helps protect your time and energy. This exercise will guide you in establishing healthy boundaries to create more balance.

1. **Instructions**:
    - Identify one area of your life where you feel overwhelmed or overcommitted (e.g., work, social obligations).
    - Write down one specific boundary you can set to protect your time and energy in this area (e.g., limiting work emails after 6 p.m., saying "no" to unnecessary commitments).
    - Practice setting and communicating this boundary over the next week.
2. **Reflection**:
    - How did setting this boundary affect your sense of balance and well-being?
    - How can continuing to set healthy boundaries improve your overall life balance?

Conclusion: Integrating These Practices into Your Life

This workbook is designed to be a companion to your journey of living with intention, cultivating mindfulness, embracing personal growth, and achieving balance. The exercises and reflections in this workbook are tools to help you apply the concepts you've learned throughout your journey. However, the real transformation comes from integrating these practices into your daily life and revisiting them consistently. Here's how you can continue to use this workbook as a living document that evolves with you:

Integrating the Practices

1. **Consistency is Key**: The power of these practices lies in repetition. Whether it's journaling about your core values, reflecting on your growth, or setting new goals, aim to integrate at least one exercise from the workbook into your daily or weekly routine.

2. **Celebrate Small Wins**: Personal growth is not a linear journey, but each step forward matters. Celebrate small victories, whether that's establishing a mindfulness practice or achieving one of your SMART goals. Reflect on these successes regularly to motivate and inspire further progress.
3. **Adjust as Needed**: Life changes, and so will your goals, priorities, and challenges. Revisit the exercises in this workbook regularly to assess where you are and what needs to shift. Allow yourself the flexibility to adapt your goals, practices, and boundaries as life evolves.
4. **Incorporate Mindfulness into Daily Life**: You don't need to set aside hours for mindfulness. Find ways to bring presence into everyday activities—whether it's through mindful listening, eating, walking, or simply pausing for a few deep breaths when feeling overwhelmed.
5. **Engage with Gratitude and Reflection**: Keep practicing gratitude, not just during the good times but especially during challenging moments. Gratitude is a practice that builds resilience, joy, and an abundant mindset. Make time for reflective journaling, using the prompts in this workbook to stay connected with your growth journey.
6. **Check-In with Your Balance**: Life will always pull you in different directions. Make it a habit to check in with your life balance using the assessments provided, and adjust your time and energy allocation when needed. Regularly setting and reviewing boundaries will help ensure that all areas of your life receive the attention they need.

Workbook Reflection: Moving Forward

As you move forward, take a moment to reflect on the following questions:
1. **What practice from this workbook resonates most with me right now, and how can I integrate it into my life today?**
2. **What changes have I noticed since I began reflecting on my core values, personal growth, and mindfulness?**
3. **How can I stay consistent with these practices to continue growing and evolving?**
4. **Which area of my life needs the most attention, and what steps can I take to bring more balance to it?**

Additional Resources

Here are a few resources you can explore to deepen your understanding and continue your journey of personal growth, intentional living, and mindfulness:

1. **Books**:
    - *The Power of Now* by Eckhart Tolle (for mindfulness and presence)
    - *Atomic Habits* by James Clear (for building sustainable habits)
    - *The Gifts of Imperfection* by Brené Brown (for cultivating self-compassion and authenticity)
2. **Online Courses and Platforms**:
    - **Headspace** or **Calm** for guided mindfulness and meditation practices.
    - **Coursera** or **edX** for lifelong learning opportunities in various fields.
    - **Insight Timer** for free meditation and mindfulness resources.
3. **Mindfulness Apps**:
    - **Ten Percent Happier**: A mindfulness app with teachings and guided meditations designed to support beginners and experienced practitioners alike.
    - **Insight Timer**: A free meditation app with thousands of guided sessions on mindfulness, gratitude, and stress reduction.

Conclusion: The Journey Continues

Remember, personal growth and intentional living are ongoing journeys—there is no fixed destination. Embrace the process, and know that every moment of presence, each reflection on your values, and every step toward your goals contributes to a more fulfilling and balanced life.

This workbook is meant to be your companion through the ups and downs, the challenges, and the triumphs. Revisit these exercises when you need guidance, adapt them as you grow, and let them serve as a reminder of your power to create the life you truly desire.

Thank you for embarking on this journey of growth, mindfulness, and intentional living. Keep moving forward with curiosity, patience, and compassion for yourself.

You've got this.

References:

The following references are influential works and leaders in the fields of mindfulness, self-care, forgiveness, spirituality, and personal development. These sources have been instrumental in shaping the ideas discussed in "Let Go 'N Live: A Guide to Releasing Stress and Finding Inner Peace."

Books

1. **Tolle, Eckhart**. *The Power of Now: A Guide to Spiritual Enlightenment.* New World Library, 2004.
   - A seminal work on mindfulness and presence, focusing on living in the present moment and finding freedom from mental overactivity.
2. **Brown, Brené**. *The Gifts of Imperfection: Let Go of Who You Think You're Supposed to Be and Embrace Who You Are.* Hazelden Publishing, 2010.
   - This book explores the importance of self-compassion, authenticity, and embracing vulnerability in the pursuit of personal growth.
3. **Clear, James**. *Atomic Habits: An Easy & Proven Way to Build Good Habits & Break Bad Ones.* Avery, 2018.
   - A practical guide on how to build sustainable habits, focused on small, incremental changes that compound over time.
4. **Dweck, Carol S.**. *Mindset: The New Psychology of Success.* Random House, 2006.
   - This book introduces the concept of the growth mindset and its importance in personal development, learning, and resilience.
5. **Kabat-Zinn, Jon**. *Wherever You Go, There You Are: Mindfulness Meditation in Everyday Life.* Hyperion, 1994.
   - One of the foundational texts on mindfulness, teaching how to cultivate presence and awareness in daily life.
6. **Emmons, Robert A.**. *Thanks!: How the New Science of Gratitude Can Make You Happier.* Houghton Mifflin Harcourt, 2007.
   - A deep dive into the science of gratitude and how cultivating a regular gratitude practice can improve mental, emotional, and physical well-being.
7. **Siegel, Daniel J.**. *The Mindful Brain: Reflection and Attunement in the Cultivation of Well-Being.* W. W. Norton & Company, 2007.
   - A neuroscience-based exploration of mindfulness and its impact on the brain, focusing on emotional regulation and self-awareness.

8. **Neff, Kristin**. *Self-Compassion: The Proven Power of Being Kind to Yourself.* HarperCollins, 2011.
    - A book that explores the concept of self-compassion and its role in emotional resilience, offering practical strategies for cultivating kindness toward oneself.

Articles and Studies

1. **Davidson, Richard J., and Jon Kabat-Zinn**. "Alterations in Brain and Immune Function Produced by Mindfulness Meditation." *Psychosomatic Medicine*, vol. 65, no. 4, 2003, pp. 564-570.
    - This study demonstrates the effects of mindfulness meditation on brain activity and immune system function, highlighting the physiological benefits of mindfulness.
2. **Fredrickson, Barbara L., et al.** "Open Hearts Build Lives: Positive Emotions, Induced Through Loving-Kindness Meditation, Build Consequential Personal Resources." *Journal of Personality and Social Psychology*, vol. 95, no. 5, 2008, pp. 1045-1062.
    - This article explores how practices like loving-kindness meditation can increase positive emotions, which in turn build personal resources such as resilience, social support, and physical health.
3. **Emmons, Robert A., and Michael E. McCullough**. "Counting Blessings Versus Burdens: An Experimental Investigation of Gratitude and Subjective Well-Being in Daily Life." *Journal of Personality and Social Psychology*, vol. 84, no. 2, 2003, pp. 377-389.
    - A groundbreaking study on the impact of gratitude practices, showing that regular gratitude journaling can lead to improved mood, well-being, and optimism.
4. **Davis, Daphne, and Jeffrey Hayes**. "What Are the Benefits of Mindfulness? A Practice Review of Psychotherapy-Related Research." *Psychotherapy*, vol. 48, no. 2, 2011, pp. 198-208.
    - This review discusses the wide range of benefits associated with mindfulness, including emotional regulation, reduced stress, and improved relationships.

Websites and Online Resources

1. **Greater Good Science Center** (University of California, Berkeley) – https://greatergood.berkeley.edu
    - Offers research-based articles and resources on gratitude, mindfulness, emotional resilience, and personal growth.
2. **Mindful.org** – https://www.mindful.org

- A comprehensive online resource for articles, guided meditations, and courses on mindfulness and presence in everyday life.
3. **Headspace** – https://www.headspace.com
    - A leading app offering guided meditations, mindfulness exercises, and tools for building resilience and reducing stress.
4. **Insight Timer** – https://insighttimer.com
    - An app providing free meditation practices, mindfulness exercises, and community support for individuals at any stage of their mindfulness journey.

Academic and Professional References

1. **Kabat-Zinn, Jon.** "Mindfulness-Based Stress Reduction (MBSR)." *American Psychological Association*, 2009.
    - A formal guide and framework for mindfulness-based stress reduction, a widely used method for improving well-being through mindfulness.
2. **Damasio, Antonio.** *Self Comes to Mind: Constructing the Conscious Brain.* Pantheon, 2010.
    - A neuroscientific exploration of how the mind and self-awareness are constructed and how mindfulness contributes to greater self-awareness and emotional regulation.
3. **Goleman, Daniel.** *Emotional Intelligence: Why It Can Matter More Than IQ.* Bantam Books, 1995.
    - This book introduced the concept of emotional intelligence (EQ) and how it plays a key role in personal growth, relationships, and success.

Closing Notes

These references offer a foundation for exploring the themes of mindfulness, personal growth, emotional resilience, and intentional living. As you continue your journey, you can revisit these resources to deepen your understanding and find practical ways to apply these concepts in your life. Each work provides valuable insights, research, and tools that can support your path to a more mindful, intentional, and fulfilling life.

Acknowledgements:

This book would not have been possible without the guidance, wisdom, and support of many individuals who have inspired me along the way.

First, I want to express my deepest gratitude to the spiritual leaders and authors whose work has profoundly shaped my understanding of mindfulness, self-compassion, and personal growth: **Thich Nhat Hanh**, **Brené Brown**, **Eckhart Tolle**, and **Jon Kabat-Zinn**. Your teachings have been a light on my own journey, and this book is a reflection of the truths you so generously share with the world.

To my family and friends, thank you for your unwavering support and encouragement. Your love has been a constant reminder of what it means to let go and live fully. You've inspired me to practice what I preach, and for that, I'm eternally grateful.

A special thank you to my mentors and teachers who have challenged me to grow, to forgive, and to embrace the ever-changing landscape of life. Your belief in me, even when I struggled to believe in myself, has made this work possible.

To my readers and those who have shared their stories of struggle and triumph with me, thank you. Your vulnerability and courage remind me that we are all on this journey together. It is for you that I wrote this book, and I hope it serves as a guide and a companion in your own pursuit of peace and freedom.

Lastly, I want to thank the universe for its endless lessons in letting go. Every challenge, every heartbreak, and every moment of uncertainty has been a teacher, offering the opportunity to grow, to heal, and to discover the true meaning of living.

To all who have been a part of this journey, directly or indirectly, thank you. This book is as much yours as it is mine.

ABOUT THE AUTHOR

Bradford M. Smith, born 1967 and raised in Lancaster County, PA, has been a polymath when it comes to life. Brad's interests range widely across business, philosophy, science, magic, arts, spirituality, engineering, mystery, fantasy, writing, psychology, wellness, sports and history.

After attending Shippensburg University for Accounting and Marketing, Brad started several independent businesses and organizations in the construction and advertising industries prior to focusing on the global franchise industry over 25 years ago with a love of small business and entrepreneurship.

When not writing, speaking, awarding franchises, consulting or just dwelling in thought, Brad enjoys the outdoors, nature, gardening, family, and the occasional cigar, while living with his wife, Judy, in West Palm Beach, FL.

Printed in Great Britain
by Amazon